高职高专
国际商务应用
系列教材

外贸英语函电

汤素娜　熊有生　刘存丰 主编
谢雨彤 副主编

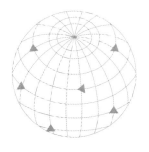

清华大学出版社
北　京

内 容 简 介

本书立足于当前外贸岗位的实际需求,适应现代信息传播方式,兼顾语言知识与沟通技巧,系统介绍了外贸英语函电写作的基本知识。本书包含了外贸业务磋商过程中各个环节往来函电的大量例文和案例,提供了函电撰写中的常用语句,可帮助学生系统掌握业务关系建立、询盘、报盘、还盘、订单处理、付款、包装与装运、售后跟进、投诉与索赔处理等工作中的函电撰写技能。

本书既可作为高等职业院校国际经济与贸易、国际商务、商务英语等相关专业的教材,也可作为从事或准备从事外贸工作的其他专业人员的培训用书。

本书封面贴有清华大学出版社防伪标签,无标签者不得销售。
版权所有,侵权必究。举报:010-62782989,beiqinquan@tup.tsinghua.edu.cn。

图书在版编目(CIP)数据

外贸英语函电/汤素娜,熊有生,刘存丰主编. —北京:清华大学出版社,2021.12(2024.8重印)
高职高专国际商务应用系列教材
ISBN 978-7-302-59828-2

Ⅰ.①外… Ⅱ.①汤… ②熊… ③刘… Ⅲ.①对外贸易－英语－电报信函－写作－高等职业教育－教材 Ⅳ.①F75

中国版本图书馆 CIP 数据核字(2021)第 271780 号

责任编辑:刘士平
封面设计:傅瑞学
责任校对:袁　芳
责任印制:曹婉颖

出版发行:清华大学出版社
网　　址:https://www.tup.com.cn,https://www.wqxuetang.com
地　　址:北京清华大学学研大厦 A 座　　邮　编:100084
社 总 机:010-83470000　　邮　购:010-62786544
投稿与读者服务:010-62776969,c-service@tup.tsinghua.edu.cn
质量反馈:010-62772015,zhiliang@tup.tsinghua.edu.cn
课件下载:https://www.tup.com.cn,010-83470410
印 装 者:三河市龙大印装有限公司
经　　销:全国新华书店
开　　本:185mm×260mm　　印　张:13.5　　字　数:326 千字
版　　次:2022 年 1 月第 1 版　　印　次:2024 年 8 月第 4 次印刷
定　　价:49.00 元

产品编号:090445-02

FOREWORD 前言

外贸英语函电是高等职业院校国际经济与贸易、国际商务、商务英语等专业的核心课程。随着信息技术的快速发展,外贸行业的信息交流方式、业务模式等情况已经与之前有了很大的不同。

党的二十大报告指出,高质量发展是全面建设社会主义现代化国家的首要任务。推动高质量发展,需要推进高水平对外开放,加快建设贸易强国。本书紧密结合信息技术发展和产业升级情况,紧密对接商务英语、电子商务、国际经济与贸易、国际商务等专业的教学标准,旨在培养适应推进高水平对外开放,加快建设贸易强国战略的外贸业务员、跨境电商运营专员、外贸助理、外贸跟单员等涉外商务人才。本书的特色主要体现在以下八个方面。

(1) 立足当前外贸岗位实际需求。本书以对外贸易岗位的函电写作任务为核心,将相关岗位所要求的不同能力进行细分,基于学生现有能力,以工作过程为导向设计学习模块。本书编者收集了福步外贸论坛、阿里巴巴国际站外贸圈等平台上的真实外贸信函范例并进行分类、整合、修改,力求使教材内容紧贴外贸工作实际。

(2) 适应现代信息传播方式,培养学生的信息素养。党的二十大报告指出,要加快发展数字经济,促进数字经济和实体经济深度融合。本书紧扣数字经济和外贸行业实体经济融合背景下,新媒体传播、多模态信息传播等趋势,围绕电子邮件系统、跨境电商平台邮箱系统等沟通工具的各项功能,增加了信息化时代下外贸函电沟通中的重要内容,包括电子邮件主题的撰写,电子邮件中文字字体、颜色选择以及文字的排版,文字与图片、视频的搭配,邮件电子签名档的设计,电子邮件的自动回复等。

(3) 语言知识与沟通技巧兼顾,提升学生的国际合作与沟通意识,培养其与国外合作伙伴进行书面商务洽谈的能力。本书通过针对性的举例,使学生了解外贸函电的撰写思路,提升语言的表达及沟通艺术,改善函电的文本结构及语言风格。

(4) 适应中国外贸相关的新产业、新业态和新商业模式。党的二十大报告指出,要建设现代化产业体系,推动制造业高端化、智能化、绿色化发展,推动共建"一带一路"高质量发展。本书立足我国外贸实践,教学内容及任务模块更多涉及高端化、智能化、绿色化的外贸产品,尽量涵盖"中国制造2025"下的重点、新兴产业,并面向包括"一带一路"市场在内的多元目标市场,力求在潜移默化中提升学生适应我国外贸产业、业态以及商业模式的函电撰写能力。

(5) 双语结合。考虑到高职学生的英语水平,本书每一模块的指导性内容主要以英文表述,力求使用较简单的词汇,生疏的词汇用中文标示其含义;而有关外贸函电沟通的技巧,则主要以中文表述为主，核心词汇用英文标示，力求为学生的阅读扫除词汇障碍，使其更好地吸收外贸函电撰写的相关知识，掌握撰写技巧。

（6）针对性强，内容贴合教学课时安排及教师的教学实际。本书范文量及练习量坚持适度原则，适合每周3～4学时，共54～72学时的教学时长，有利于满足教师教学所需，也有利于缓解学生在函电课程学习中的畏多畏难心理。

（7）坚持任务导向、成果导向。本书将每一模块分成若干任务，通过各种仿真任务驱动，调动学生参与，使学生完成真实的函电撰写实践任务，掌握外贸相关工作岗位的函电撰写能力。

（8）渗透课程思政。党的二十大报告指出，育人的根本在于立德。要全面贯彻党的教育方针，落实立德树人根本任务，培养德智体美劳全面发展的社会主义建设者和接班人。本书坚持教学与价值引领相结合，在模板设计、内容选择以及实操活动的布置等方面，凸显课程思政，力求使学习者能遵守职业道德，具备较强的服务意识，具备一定的国际化视野、跨文化交际意识，具备较强的沟通能力、应变能力，具备较强的信息获取能力、学习能力以及"互联网＋"思维，成为精益求精、有能力、善沟通、高素养的服务型工匠。

本书由汤素娜、熊有生、刘存丰担任主编，谢雨彤担任副主编，具体编写分工如下：模块2、模块5由广东行政职业学院汤素娜编写；模块3由广东行政职业学院汤素娜、高颖欣编写；模块4由广东行政职业学院汤素娜、翟映华编写；模块1、模块11由广州铁路职业技术学院熊有生编写；模块6、模块7由广州科技贸易职业学院刘存丰编写；模块10由广东行政职业学院谢雨彤编写；模块8由广东工程职业技术学院黄玲玲和广州城建职业学院孙开来编写；模块9由汤素娜、刘存丰编写；由汤素娜负责总纂与定稿。

本书是国家终身教育智慧教育平台数字化学习资源及广东行政职业学院院级在线开放课程"外贸英语函电"的配套教材，可在智慧职教平台"慕课学院"中搜索课程名称观看。同时，本书配套资源丰富，包括课程标准、教案、教学课件、习题库等数字资源，方便教师及学生使用。

感谢广州市大洋信息技术股份有限公司等企业为本书的编写提出了宝贵的建议。在编写过程中，我们参阅了大量的资料及网络信息，在此一并表示感谢。由于编者水平有限，本书难免有疏漏或不妥之处，欢迎使用本书的读者朋友们批评、指正。

编　者

2024年8月

CONTENTS 目 录

Module 1　Fundamentals of Business Writing
模块 1　外贸函电写作的基本要义 ·· 1
　　Task 1　Writing a Business Letter ·· 1
　　Task 2　Writing a Business Email ·· 8
　　Task 3　Principles of Business Writing ·· 12

Module 2　Establishing Business Relations
模块 2　建立业务关系 ··· 26
　　Task 1　Writing a Sales Email ··· 26
　　Task 2　Writing to Follow-up ··· 37

Module 3　Inquiries
模块 3　询盘 ·· 46
　　Task 1　Writing an Inquiry ·· 46
　　Task 2　Replying to Inquiries ··· 52

Module 4　Offers
模块 4　报盘 ·· 62
　　Task 1　Making an Offer ·· 62
　　Task 2　Following up after Making an Offer ··································· 70

Module 5　Counter-offers
模块 5　还盘 ·· 77
　　Task 1　Writing a Counter-offer to the Seller ··································· 77
　　Task 2　Writing a Re-counteroffer to the Buyer ································ 81
　　Task 3　Following up after Replying to the Buyer's Counter-offer ············ 88

Module 6　Dealing with Orders
模块 6　订单处理 ··· 97
Task 1　Responding to Orders ··· 97
Task 2　Preparing Pre-production Samples ································ 103

Module 7　Payment
模块 7　付款 ··· 110
Task 1　Negotiating Terms of Payment ·· 113
Task 2　Dealing with Letter of Credit ··· 118
Task 3　Settling Other Payment Problems ···································· 123

Module 8　Packing, Shipment and Insurance
模块 8　包装、装运和保险 ·· 131
Task 1　Writing on Packing Requirements ··································· 131
Task 2　Writing on Shipment Arrangement ································· 139
Task 3　Writing on Insurance Arrangement ································· 147

Module 9　After-sales Follow-up
模块 9　售后跟进 ·· 158
Task 1　Asking for Feedback ·· 158
Task 2　Introducing Latest Products ·· 162
Task 3　Offering Discounts ··· 165

Module 10　Complaints and Claims
模块 10　投诉与索赔 ··· 171
Task 1　Writing and Replying to Complaints ································ 171
Task 2　Writing and Replying to Claims ····································· 178

Module 11　Miscellaneous Correspondence
模块 11　其他函电 ·· 188
Task 1　Setting Email Auto Replies ·· 188
Task 2　Writing Notifications ··· 194
Task 3　Greetings on Special Occasions ······································ 202

参考文献 ··· 209

Module 1 Fundamentals of Business Writing

模块❶ 外贸函电写作的基本要义

Learning Goals

❖ Know about the basic structure and format of business letters and emails.
❖ Get familiar with the 7C writing principles in business correspondence and be able to revise messages based on them.
❖ Be able to apply proper structure, format and writing principles to actual business correspondence.

Lead-in

Situation: You're a salesperson. You're now given a task to write an email to your client.
Questions:
1. Do you think you can write randomly, or need to follow some kinds of format?
2. What are the general purposes of business writing? To fulfill these purposes, which principles shall we follow?

Task 1 Writing a Business Letter

The structure and format of business letters are constantly changing in international trade. For instance, with the degree of familiarity increasing between trade partners, business letters become less formal than before. However, there are still some usual practices that should be followed in terms of structure and format.

外贸英语函电

Section 1 Structure of a Business Letter

Sample

A well-constructed business letter is often made up of the parts structured in the following way.

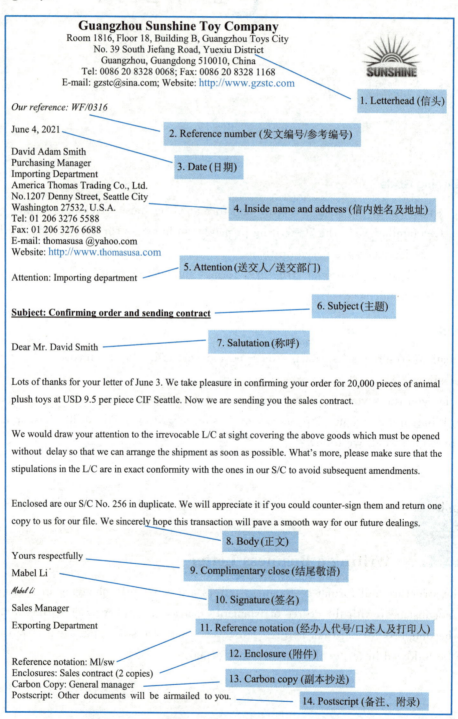

Module 1 Fundamentals of Business Writing
模块1 外贸函电写作的基本要义

Usually, there are fourteen parts in a standard business letter. However, only seven of them are necessary for a daily business letter.

Necessary Parts	Optional Parts
Letterhead	Reference number
Date	Attention
Inside name and address	Subject
Salutation	Reference notation
Body	Enclosure
Complimentary close	Carbon copy
Signature	Postscript

1. Letterhead（信头）

A business letterhead is a pre-printed heading on documents like letters, memos, and notes. The heading is centered at the top of the letter; sometimes it is in the top-right corner or the top-left corner. Usually, companies use printed paper with a heading at the top.

The heading can create a typical identity or vivid image of a company. It bears basic information of the company such as name, logo, address, postcode, telephone number, fax number, email, website, etc.

An Example of Heading
China Petroleum Guangzhou Branch Room 3802, Floor 38, Petroleum Building, No. 198 East Xiaogang Road, Haizhu District, Guangzhou, Guangdong 510541, China Tel: +86 208566 8590; Fax: +86 8566 8592 mail: cpgzb@sina.com Website: cpgzpetrol.com.cn

2. Reference number（发文编号/参考编号）

Reference number always appears on the left margin with one or two lines below the letterhead, no matter which format is used.

A reference number is often used for identifying, filing and tracing back in the future. It usually contains departmental code, chronological number, etc.

It is generally marked "Our ref: " and "Your ref: " to avoid confusion.

Our ref: WF/0604 Your ref: DF0905	Our ref: WF/ml0604 Your ref: DF/ds0905

3. Date（日期）

The date is often located below the reference number with one or two lines; it appears

3

on the left margin or in the middle right.

The date provides the evidence or reference of time when the letter is written; it consists of day, month and year. The format of the date according to the following table.

Recommended	October 12,2019	12 October 2019	
Acceptable, but not Recommended	October 12th,2019	12th October 2019	Oct. 12,2019 Oct. 12th,2019
Not Acceptable	2019/10/12 2019-10-12 2019. 10. 12 19/10/12	10/12/2019 10-12-2019 10. 12. 2019 10/12/19	October,12th,2019 October,12,2019

4. Inside name and address（信内姓名及地址）

It begins with one or two lines below the date and should always be left justified, no matter which format is used.

It includes the receiver's basic information such as name, address, telephone number, email, etc.

Example 1	Example 2
David Smith Purchasing Manager Importing Department America Thomas Trading Co., Ltd. No. 1207 Denny Street Seattle City Washington 27532 The U. S. A.	Ms. Jane Smith Sales Manager Textile Import and Export Corporation No. 31 West Green Street Florida 33402 The U. S. A.

5. Attention（送交人/送交部门）

The attention line is placed on the left margin with one or two lines below the inside name and address.

This part is not a must in official or business letters. It is used when the writer wishes to lead the letter to a particular person or department when the letter is addressed to a company.

Below are some examples.

(1) Attention: Mr. David Smith, Purchasing Manager.

(2) ATTN: Mr. David Smith, Purchasing Manager.

(3) For the attention of Mr. David Smith, Purchasing Manager.

(4) Attention: Importing Department.

6. Subject（主题）

The subject is often located either on the left margin or in the middle with one or two lines below the attention line, but sometimes it can be set in the middle below the salutation with one or two-line space.

It calls the receiver's attention to the topic of the letter, and it can also serve as a guide for filing.

The subject may be emphasized by underlining, using **bold font**, *italicized* or CAPITAL LETTERS. Here are some examples.

（1）Subject：**Confirming Order and Sending Contract**
（2）Subject：*Confirming Order and Sending Contract*
（3）Subject：Confirming Order and Sending Contract
（4）Subject：CONFIRMING ORDER AND SENDING CONTRACT

("Subject" is also written as SUBJECT; Sub.; Re.; SUB; RE.)

7. Salutation（称呼）

The salutation follows the subject line below one line. It is always left-justified, no matter which format is adopted. It is used to greet the receiver and show politeness. It usually begins with "Dear" followed by the receiver's name with the official title, job title or professional title if any.

8. Body（正文）

The body is often positioned either on the left margin or indented four-letter to the right. It appears one or two lines below the salutation. It is the most important part of a business letter because it expresses the writer's ideas, opinions, purposes, wishes, etc. It includes three parts: opening, middle and closing. The body is the main part of a letter, and therefore should be carefully planned.

9. Complimentary close（结尾敬语）

It appears below the last paragraph of the body with one or two-line space. It can convey the writer's courtesy and respect to the receiver. As a polite way of ending the letter, it should match the form of salutation and the signature.

The following examples show the matching punctuation between the salutation and complimentary close.

Punctuation	With comma "," (Britain English)	With colon ":" (American English)	Without punctuation
Salutation	Dear Mr. David Smith,	Dear Mr. David Smith:	Dear Mr. David Smith
Complimentary close	Yours respectfully, Mabel Li	Yours respectfully, Mabel Li	Yours respectfully Mabel Li

10. Signature（签名）

The signature is located below complimentary close leaving one or two lines, whether it should be left-justified or in the middle right depends on the format the writer has selected. The signature gives authority to the contents of the letter or confirms the legal power of the letter.

Signature Example
Mabel Li
Mabel Li
Sales Manager
Guangzhou Sunshine Toy Company

11. Reference notation（经办人代号/口述人及打印人）

The reference notation is placed on the left margin with one or two-line space below the signature. It indicates who should take the responsibility for the letter if any dispute happens. It shows the initials of the person who dictated the letter and the initials of the typist or secretary who typed the letter.

Note：

The dictator's name and the typist's name are divided by a slash "/" or colon ":".

For example, if the dictator is Mabel Li and the typist is Susan Wu, we may write in the following format.

ML/SW；ML：SW   ML/sw；ML：sw   ml/sw；ml：sw

12. Enclosure（附件）

The enclosure appears on the left margin with one or two-line space below the signature. It reminds the receiver that there are documents attached to the letter. Here are the examples.

Enclosure/Encl/Enc：Sales contract （1 copy）

Enclosures/Encls/Encs：Sales contract （2 copies）

13. Carbon copy（副本抄送）

The carbon copy is positioned on the left margin below the enclosure with one or two lines. It informs the receiver that this letter has been sent to someone else at the same time. If you do not want the receiver to know to whom else you send this letter, you can use the function of "b.c.c." (short for "blind carbon copy") to send the copies.

Carbon Copy	Blind Carbon Copy
Copy to Mr. Stephen/General Manager CC：Mr. Stephen/General Manager （Cc, cc）	BCC：Mr. Stephen/General Manager （Bcc, bcc）
Copy to Guangzhou Sunshine Toy Company CC：Guangzhou Sunshine Toy Company （Cc, cc）	BCC：Guangzhou Sunshine Toy Company （Bcc, bcc）

14. Postscript（备注、附录）

The postscript is left-justified following carbon copy by one or two lines.

It is used deliberately to draw the reader's attention to a point the writer wishes to emphasize or something he forgets to mention.

Example：

P. S. ：*The sample will be mailed to you within three days.*

Section 2　Layout of a Business Letter

Usually，the way of laying out a letter includes line spacing，indenting（缩进），underlining，CAPITALIZING and so on. Although formality in modern business letters tends to become less conventional（传统的）and more conversational（非正式的），it still follows a more or less set pattern determined by custom. Many business companies adopt a particular format or layout of a letter and standardize it throughout the entire organization.

(1) **Full Block Style**（most often used）	(2) **Modified Block Style**（also popular）	(3) **Indented Style**（an older format, less popular now）
The whole text or part is aligned or starts from the left margin. Paragraphs are single-spaced, not indented, but with a double space between paragraphs.	A modified block differs from full block style in that the date and signature lines begin at the centre of the page line.	New paragraphs are indented to the right of the left margin. Other parts are moved farther to the right half of the page.

Task 2

Writing a Business Email

Compared with traditional letters, an email has the advantages of convenient sending and receiving, fast delivery, wide communication objects, free delivery, safe and easy to save. Emails have greatly facilitated communications and exchanges in business circles.

Sample

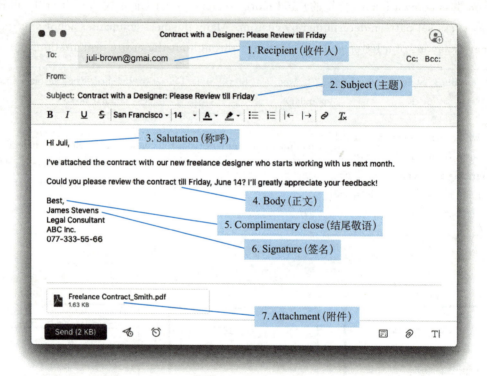

1. **Recipient (收件人)**

(1) To multiple recipients, the writer can separate them by using a comma (,) or a semicolon (;).

(2) CC. CC means carbon copy. When an email is copied to one or more recipients, both the main recipient (whose address is in the "To:" field) and the CC'd recipients (whose address is in the "CC:" field) can see all the addresses to which the message was sent.

(3) BCC. When a message is blind carbon copied, neither the main recipient nor the BCC'd recipients can see the addresses in the "BCC:" field.

2. Subject（主题）

The subject line often determines whether an email is opened and how the recipient responds. The followings are some tips on how to write the subject of an email.

（1）Always write a subject. Although the email system allow us to send an email without a subject, an email with a blank subject line may be deleted, lost, or may immediately irritate the recipient, who is forced to open the email to figure out what it's about.

（2）Keep it short. A typical inbox reveals about 60 characters of an email's subject line, while a mobile phone shows just 25 to 30 characters. Nowadays emails are very often opened on mobile devices, which means longer subject lines will get cut off. The writer should get right to the point in about 6－8 words.

（3）Write a clear and specific topic. The subject line should communicate exactly what the email is about so that the recipient can prioritize the email's importance. Avoid writing generic and vague subject lines; instead, try to make them short but informative.

Not Recommended	Recommended
Subject：Proposal	Subject：Product XYZ Case Study Proposal
Subject：Electronic Toys Conference	Subject：Invitation of Electronic Toys Conference, Guangzhou Aug. 14－16

（4）Ask for a response. If you need a response, make it clear in the subject line by saying "please reply" or "thoughts needed on ×××topic". If not, simply start the line with "Please read" or add an "FYI" to the end.

（5）Set a deadline in the subject line, if necessary. For example, after the email's topic, you could say: "Please reply by Friday."

3. Salutation（称呼）

The salutation is also left-justified. It could be the receiver's name with the official title, job title, etc. Please refer to Task 1.

4. Body（正文）

The body of a formal email typically elaborates on the purpose of the email. Although the body contains detailed information, it's important to write clearly and concisely. Another important aspect is choosing the right font, size, color, and spacing.

For writing emails in English, here is the list of some web safe fonts—aka email safe fonts—that the writer may use with a 100% guarantee that they will render in recipients' inboxes as planned: Arial, Times New Roman, Verdana, Courier New, Tahoma, Georgia.

The writer should keep the number of colors to the minimum, with no more than 3 colors in an email. Use a **bold font**, a different font, red color or CAPITAL LETTERS only when we want to highlight one sentence or a phrase. Here's an example.

> Hi!
>
> Thanks for ordering our thermal bottles! We're offering a coupon code to use at **Weichi Shop**.
>
> Use coupon code **IMNEW** for **30% OFF**!

5. Complimentary close(结尾敬语)

The closing the writer choose should match the tone of the rest of the email. Formal closings include "Sincerely" and "Thank you" while less formal messages can use "Cheers" "Talk to you soon!" or "See you later!" (This is similar to a business letter. Please refer to Task 1 for more details.)

6. Signature（签名）

An email might be signed off with the writer's name (first and last name), title, company name, etc.

Many email systems allow us to add a signature block (签名档, a personalized block of text automatically appended at the bottom of an email message) to every email we create.

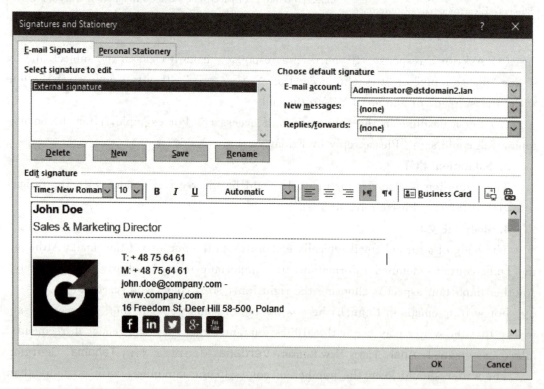

Setting a signature block in Outlook

A professional email signature block usually contains information such as:
- First name and last name.
- Title or position.

- Company name.
- Contact information: phone number, email address, etc.
- Links to the company's social media platforms.
- A company logo.
- A headshot (头像).

Examples of the signature block

A strong email signature is attention-getting but also professional. It's not flashy, but not bland either. The followings are some tips.

- Limit your signature to three or four lines of text. Too many lines of text will make it overstuffed, and painful for the recipient to read on a mobile device.
- Include a colored image (the writer's headshot or logo of the company). People remember visuals better than text.

There are some free email signature generators (签名档生成器) available online to help create professional email signatures.

7. Attachment (附件)

Email attachments are files that are attached to email messages, thereby increasing the potential value or benefit of that message to the recipient. These may be files of different formats, sizes, and contents. Attachments can be in text files, documents, spreadsheets, and PDF forms.

In the body of the email message, the writer should tell the recipient whether an attachment is included. Even if the only important matter is the attached file, the writer should make the recipient aware of the files and write briefly what each file is about by saying:

- *Please find the attached … (sales report/proposal/quotation/picture/price-list) for … (your review/reference/approval/records/signature).*
- *Please find the attached file you requested.*
- *Please check the attachment for details.*
- *The attached … shows …*
- *I have attached …*
- *The attached … includes …*

Tips on attachments are as below.

(1) The use of the word "enclosed" is inappropriate in electronic media. (The word "enclosed" is used in paper mails.)

(2) Avoid attaching very heavy files to an email, unless very necessary. It could be frustrating for the recipient to download.

(3) In cases we need to send any attachments, it is important to mention in the body of the email message how many files are attached.

More tips on writing a business email are as below.

(1) To make it easier for the recipient to put the email in folders, the writer should avoid unrelated matters. The writer may send separate emails for different matters. Don't hijack a thread on one topic to discuss another topic. Start a new email thread instead.

(2) Use "Reply All" only when truly needed. No one likes the person who clogs the inbox.

(3) Retain the thread（电子邮件线程）. When responding to an email, include previous messages and add the response to the top. An email thread is an email message that includes a running list of all the succeeding replies starting with the original email. The thread is useful for the readers to check what has been discussed.

Principles of Business Writing

As we all know, business writing is very important in international trade because it can help establish business relations, ask for or convey business information, make or accept an offer, place an order and settle complaints, claims, etc. To some extent, a successful business transaction greatly depends on how well a business letter is written. Although nowadays business writing tends to be less conventional and more conversational in style, there are still some principles that should be strictly followed.

Generally, there are seven principles in business writing, which are usually called "Seven-C Principles". They are completeness, concreteness, clearness, conciseness, correctness, courtesy and consideration.

1. Completeness（完整性）

Completeness means that a business letter must cover all necessary information and relevant data that readers would like to know. For example, if we are writing to invite someone to take part in an activity, we need to clarify *who*, *what*, *when*, *where*, *why*, and *how*. On the other hand, an incomplete letter is annoying and time-consuming, because it requires more time to call for further correspondence to clarify the point. Besides, an incomplete letter may result in loss of goodwill, sales and valued customers.

Module 1 Fundamentals of Business Writing
模块 1 外贸函电写作的基本要义

Tips:

(1) Provide all necessary information.

(2) Answer precisely all questions asked.

(3) Give something extra when desirable.

Incomplete Expression	Complete Expression
I would like to sincerely invite you to the product fair.	I would like to sincerely invite you to the product fair, which will kick off in Guangzhou International Exhibition Center at 9:00 a.m. on March 10.

2. Concreteness(具体性)

Concreteness means that a business letter should be specific, definite and vivid rather than vague, general and abstract. A successful business letter should avoid emptiness in content and vagueness in the idea. When writing letters, the writer can use vivid words, specific figures and detailed facts so that readers may understand correctly.

Tips:

(1) Use precise modifiers and mention specific facts, figures and dates.

(2) Use the active verb or voice.

(3) Choose vivid words.

We can use the following method to avoid vague modifiers.

Vague Modifiers	How to Avoid Vague Modifiers
as soon as possible	State an exact date or time.
better	Provide specific information.
big	State the size or measurement.
fast	State the exact rate of speed.
few	State a number.
good	Describe fully.
high	State the exact height.
little	Describe the size.
long	State the distance or measurement.
many	State a number.
more	State the difference in numbers.
most	Quote an exact number or percentage.
several	State a number.
slow	State the exact rate of speed.

Here are some examples.

Vague Expressions	Specific and Precise Expressions
We suffered from a significant loss	We suffered from an 80% loss.
The majority of our customers are satisfied with our products.	Our survey reveals that 91% of our customers are satisfied with our products.
Thank you for your order.	Thanks for your order No. 126 for robot cleaners.
Many thanks for your beautiful gift.	Many thanks for the beautiful scarf.
We wish to confirm our sales contract sent yesterday.	We wish to confirm our sales contract sent on July 10.
Our new product will arrive soon.	Please return the form by Monday, June 12.
Please return the form as soon as possible	Our new product arrives October 1.

3. Clearness（清晰性）

Clearness means that a business letter must be clear and easy to understand. That is to say, the writers should express their meaning clearly so that the readers can understand it well.

Tips：

（1）Avoid using words with multiple or unclear meanings.

（2）Pay attention to the position of modifiers.

（3）Pay attention to the sentence structure.

（4）Don't put more than one idea in a sentence.

（5）Don't put more than one topic in a paragraph.

（6）Don't put more than one subject in a letter.

Here we present several examples.

Unclear Sentences	Clear Sentences
As to the steamers sailing from Shenzhen to Toronto, we have bi-monthly direct sailing services. (note: "twice a month" or "once two months"?)	We have two direct sailings every month from Shenzhen to Toronto. We have a direct sailing every two months from Shenzhen to Toronto.
We shall be able to supply 10 cases of sports shoes only.	We shall be able to supply only 10 cases of sports shoes.
We sent you 4 samples of the goods as requested in your email of May 6 by air.	We sent you 4 samples of the goods by air as requested in your email of May 6.
Mr. Li wrote to Mr. Hunter that he had received his order. (Note: Who is "he"?)	Mr. Li wrote to Mr. Hunter that he had received Mr. Hunter's order.
Please let us know what you wish us to do about this matter as soon as possible.	Please let us know as soon as possible what you wish us to do about this matter.

4. Conciseness(简洁性)

Conciseness means that a business letter should express a great deal of information in just a few words. In other words, a concise letter should be straightforward, specific and accurate. To achieve this effect, the writer should try to avoid wordy expressions and unnecessary repetitions. However, remember never to seek brevity at the expense of clearness, courtesy and completeness. Sometimes a letter dealing with a complaint or claim must be long in sentences and complicated in structure.

Tips:

(1) Eliminate wordy expressions.

(2) Delete irrelevant words and phrases.

(3) Use words to replace phrases or sentences.

(4) Do not use rambling sentences.

(5) Use single words in place of phrases.

(6) Include only relevant material.

Here are some examples for concise expression.

Avoid Inefficient Words and Phrases	Use Efficient Words and Phrases
as a matter of fact	in fact; indeed
at that point in time	then
at this time; at this point in time	now
during the month of May	during May
for the amount of $550	for $550
in accordance with your suggestion	as you suggested
at the present time	now
come to a decision	decide
for the purpose of	for
for the reason that	since, because
in accordance with	according to
in an efficient manner	efficiently
in the near future	soon
owing to the fact that; because of the fact that	because

Avoid Inefficient Sentences	Use Efficient Sentences
Unfortunately, we have stopped producing this type of camera <u>for the reason that</u> its sales were rather low.	Unfortunately, we have stopped producing this type of camera <u>because</u> its sales were rather low.

Continued

Avoid Inefficient Sentences	Use Efficient Sentences
As per your request, please find enclosed herewith a check in the amount of $16.	As requested, I am enclosing a check for $16.
We require a full-automatic washing machine which is of the new type.	We require a new-type full-automatic washing machine.
I would like to take this opportunity to tell you that we are grateful to you.	Thank you.

5. Correctness（正确性）

Correctness means that a business letter must be free from improper punctuation, misspelled words, poor grammar and badly constructed sentences. Moreover, it should be accurate in such information as product name, specification, quantity, size, color, unit price, etc. Correctness is the basis of all business letters, for it concerns the rights, obligations and interests of both trade parties.

Tips:

Check the correctness of the statement, numerical expressions, commercial terms, grammar, word spelling and punctuation, etc.

Incorrect Spelling or Usage	Correct Spelling or Usage
I am please to accept your quotation for our caping machine.	I am pleased to accept your quotation for our capping machine.
Our products are much lower in prices than other.	Our products are much lower in prices than others.
The two first items are not available at present.	The first two items are not available at present.

6. Courtesy（礼貌）

Courtesy means that a business letter should be polite, sincere and thoughtful. That means the writer should use a polite tone, words, phrases and show a sincere attitude. Besides, punctuality is essential to politeness and a prompt reply is always more valued than a delayed one. However, when courtesy conflicts with conciseness, we should sacrifice conciseness without losing politeness.

Tips:

(1) Use "We-attitude" if the news or information is **bad** for your business partners.

If the recipient's behavior produces **negative** effects, the writer had better select the **passive voice** to avoid placing specific blame on someone. On the other hand, when describing someone's **positive** behavior, it's better to use **an active voice**.

Module 1 Fundamentals of Business Writing
模块 1 外贸函电写作的基本要义

You-attitude or Passive Voice	We-attitude or Active Voice
You did not make payment on time.	We did not receive the payment on time.
You failed to open the L/C on time.	We did not receive the L/C up to now.
You made a very careless mistake.	We found that there was a careless mistake.
You failed to enclose a cheque.	A cheque was not enclosed.
You cannot have a discount at this time.	I'm afraid a discount can not be given at this time.
You made a very careless mistake during shipment.	A careless mistake was made during shipment.
Your complaint is being looked into.	We are looking into your complaint.
The new model was designed by our technicians.	Our technicians designed the new model.

(2) Use mitigation（缓和的语气）.

Use "we are afraid" "we would say" "we may (or might) say" "we (would) think" "it seems (or would seem) to us" "we (would) suggest".

Without Mitigation	With Mitigation
We cannot comply with your request.	We are afraid we cannot comply with your request.
Our products are the very best on the market.	We might say that our products are the very best on the market.
We have not yet had your reply.	It appears that we have not yet had your reply.

(3) Use positive tones, words and phrases instead of negative ones.

Negative	Positive
You failed to give us the specifications of the sofa that you ordered.	Will you please give us the specifications of the sofa that you ordered?
We will not compensate for your loss because we did not receive enough evidence.	You will be compensated for your loss if you can provide us with enough evidence.
Your letter is not clear at all; I cannot understand it.	Perhaps you could write your letter clearly and then I can understand it correctly.
We do not make exchanges（换货）without receipts.	With your receipt, you may exchange your purchase.
Lucy, you made serious mistakes in your report.	Lucy, please recheck the accuracy of your report.

(4) Use polite words and forms.

Change command tone（命令语气）into requesting tone（请求语气）; change imperative sentences（祈使句）into general questions（一般疑问句）.

17

Command Tone, Imperative Sentences	Requesting Tone, General Questions
You ought to tell us more detailed information about your requirement.	Will you please let us know more detailed information about your requirement?
You ought to accept the terms of payment as stipulated in S/C.	It seems better for you to accept the terms of payment as stipulated in S/C.
We would like you to ship the goods before July 1.	Would you please ship the goods before July 1?
We will have to cancel your order because you fail to open the L/C in time.	Would you tell us if there is something that prevents you from establishing the L/C?
As we opened the L/C two months ago, just arrange to ship the goods immediately!	As we opened the L/C two months ago, we would be grateful if you could arrange to ship the goods immediately.

Use past subjunctive(虚拟的) form.
- **Would** you send us your latest catalogue and price list?
- We **would** ask you to make a prompt shipment.
- We wish you **would** let us have a reply soon.

7. Consideration（为收件人着想）

Consideration means that a business letter should be reader-oriented. That is to say, writers should think from readers' points of view, respect readers' feelings and understand readers' difficulties in their places. Consideration is an often-used principle and native English writers attach great importance to it because it is helpful to avoid awkward situations and promote cooperation.

Tips:

(1) Use "You-attitude" if the news or information is **good** for your business partners.

(2) Provide elements of interest or desire.

(3) Highlight positive and pleasant facts.

Command Tone, Imperative Sentences	Requesting Tone, General Questions
We have sent the products to you this morning.	You will receive the products tomorrow afternoon.
We sell this bag for the lowest price of £6 each and suggest a retail price of £8.	You can reap a £2 profit on each bag that you sell at £8, for your cost is only £6.
We warmly welcome you to New York.	You are warmly welcome to New York.
I am happy to inform you that we have approved your loan.	Congratulations! Your loan has been approved.

Tips

商务信函写作的注意事项

商务信函一般包括"BME"三个模块,即:B—开头(Beginning),M—中间(Middle),E—结尾(End)。出于不同的撰写目的,需要往 BME 三部分里填充不同的内容。

一般来说,商务信函写作应重视以下几点。

(1) 明确写信目的。一般来说,商务信函写作的目的有:Information(提供信息)、Sales or persuasion(销售、说服)、Request(请求)、Complain(投诉)和 Goodwill(示好)等。我们为何写信?我们期望收件人看完后做什么?这些都是写信前必须思考的问题。

(2) 分析收件人。充分了解收件人有助于更精准地表达意愿并选择适当的用语。

(3) 表达简洁。较为理想的效果是收件人在花几秒钟浏览之后,就能获取我们希望他了解的信息,知道我们的意图以及他自己需要做什么。长篇大论容易使繁忙的商务人士望而生畏。

(4) 使用简单的语言。商务信函的写作与文学作品的写作不一样,商务信函一定要让人快速读懂。信件的语言应干净利落,避免使用冗句,即使是正式的信函,也是讲清楚即可,不要使用过多套话。

(5) 遵循格式。商业信函有其特定格式,即使是非正式的电子邮件,也要遵循一定的格式。

(6) 检查。写完之后检查是否有内容错误、语法错误、拼写错误等。如果信函非常重要,最好请同事再检查一次。

(7) 三思而后"发送"。如果不是特别着急的邮件,写完之后不妨先放一放,过一会儿再读一遍,分析一下表达是否明确,语气是否妥当,思考之后可进行适当调整。

Communication Laboratory

I. Put the following components in the letter. Some have been done for you.

Body(正文)	Postscript(备注、附录)	Carbon copy(副本抄送)
Salutation(称呼)	Enclosure(附件)	Subject(主题)
Reference number(发文编号)	Attention(送交人)	Signature(签名)
Inside name and address(信内姓名及地址)	Letterhead(信头)	
Date(日期)	Complimentary close(结尾敬语)	

Letterhead(信头)

Reference number(发文编号)

Inside name and address
(信内姓名及地址)

Attention(送交人)

Reference notation：LF/sy
Carbon copy(副本抄送)
Enclosure(附件)
Postscript(备注、附录)

II. Translate the following parts into English.

1. 信头

广州阳光服装有限公司 中国广州市天河区天河北路 172 号 城启大厦 26 层 电话：0086 20 2233 5789 传真：0086 20 2244 5789 网址：www.gzsclothes.com.cn 电子邮箱：gzsclothes@gzsunshine.com	

2. 发文编号/参考编号

我方参考编号：WF2105SL	

3. 日期

2021 年 5 月 13 日	

4. 送交人、部门/主办人、部门

卢卡斯先生，市场部经理	

5. 主题

迷你风扇的最新商品目录和报价单	

6. 附件

产品目录及报价单	

III. Rewrite the following sentences so that they are positive rather than negative in tone.

1. You cannot visit the plant on Sunday.
2. Unfortunately, your order cannot be shipped until next week.
3. Your negligence in this matter caused damage to the equipment.
4. We regret to inform you that we cannot permit you to use Room 806 for your meeting on Saturday, as Mr. Stephen asked for it first. We can, however, let you use

Room 908, but it seats only 60.

5. Our office will be closed at 6:00 p.m.

IV. Rewrite the following sentences by using the You-attitude.

1. We will be pleased to deliver your order by May 5.

2. We have worked for 10 years to develop the best model car for our customers.

3. I am pleased to inform you that I can grant a 5% discount for your purchase of toys.

4. We have shipped the Dove desk set you ordered on May 3.

5. Our rich experience in export sales has enabled us to provide the best service.

V. Use concrete words to replace the italicized ones in the following sentences.

1. If we do not receive the goods *soon*, we will cancel the order.

2. Damage from the fire was *significant*.

3. We will need some new equipment *soon*.

VI. Rewrite the following sentences to make them more concise in wording.

1. Losses caused by the strike exceed the amount of $368 000.

2. Reference is made to your letter of May 15, in which you requested us to send a quotation to you without delay.

3. As per your request, I am enclosing a check for the amount of USD 90.50.

4. I want to take this opportunity to tell you that we are grateful to you.

5. We express our regret at being unable to fulfill your order on this occasion.

6. Please make an agreement to purchase the Marco system.

VII. The following are two pairs of business letters. Compare and tell which one is better and why.

Letter 1 - a

Dear Mr. Crane:

We are in receipt of and would like to thank you for your email and attached catalog of June 14. After close examination, we have come to the conclusion that your products are of no interest to us, but we wish you every success in your future business.

Sincerely yours,
Linda

Module 1   Fundamentals of Business Writing
模块 1   外贸函电写作的基本要义

Letter 1 – b

Dear Mr. Crane:

Thank you for your catalog sent on June 14. We appreciate your interest in our company though your products fall out of our line for the time being. We wish you every success in your future business.

Sincerely yours,
Linda

Letter 2 – a

Subject: REMINDER!!!

Dear Sir:

I would appreciate it if you would bear in mind that I am no longer responsible for dealing with sales activities in the North American region. Some of your staff keep sending inquiries to me, but the responsibility for dealing with inquiries has been taken over by Fred Deng. He is the one who should be contacted henceforth for inquiries and orders.

Your cooperation is appreciated in making sure all your staffs know about this.

BRgs/Alisa

Letter 2 – b

Subject: Your Inquiries for Toys

Dear Mr. Smiths:

Some of your staff are still sending inquiries for toys to me. However, the responsibility for dealing with inquiries has been taken over by Fred Deng since last month. Please inform your staff to contact Fred (email: Fred_deng@atd.com, mobile: 86 1367522421) from now on.

Thank you for your help.

Best regards,
Alisa

VIII. **Each pair of the following statements expresses the same idea. According to the criteria for effective business writing discussed in this module, which one do you think is more appropriate?**

1. Remind somebody to submit his business report.

   a. Don't forget to submit your business report by July 3.

   b. Remember to submit your business report by July 3.

2. Reply to a letter, which did not provide the specifications of some goods ordered.

   a. Please send the complete specifications for Order No. 324, so we can complete it on time.

   b. You neglected to indicate the specifications for Order No. 324.

3. Request a business partner to effect payment.

   a. Would you please pay this amount as soon as you can at Bank of China, Liaoning?

   b. We hope that you can pay this amount to us as soon as possible.

4. Refer to the job completed.

   a. The job was completed ahead of time.

   b. Armando completed the job ahead of time.

5. Decline your business partner's request for cash.

   a. We regret to inform you that we must deny your request for cash.

   b. We are very sorry that we can pay you only on a credit basis.

6. Talk about coverage（投保范围）issue.

   a. This coverage issue needs attention soon.

   b. Please call me at 86 13512345678 before the end of the month so that we can discuss the situation and decide how to proceed.

7. Introduce our company.

   a. At Lanyue Cleaners, you'll find services to meet all your dry cleaning needs. For three generations, our goal has been to treat your clothes as if they were our own.

   b. We at Lanyue Cleaners provide the best dry cleaning around. We're in our third generation. Our quality speaks for itself.

8. Introduce the goal of the committee.

   a. The committee has been organized and set up to provide leadership in our effort to improve our abilities to communicate in and between departmental structures.

   b. The committee's goal is to improve communication between all departments.

IX. **Write an email in English based on the situation given.**

Suppose you're a sales representative. You are asked to write an email to invite Mr. Thomas Smiths(email address: thomas_smiths@detek.com) to a business dinner. You'd like to CC the email to Mrs. Amy Florence(amy_florence@detek.com) and BCC to Mr. Wang Fei(wangfei@gzsunshine.com). Your email should contain necessary information about the event and your email should follow the 7C writing principles. You also attach an invitation letter to this email. Please provide details of the event by yourself.

To	
Cc	
Bcc	

Remove Cc - Remove Bcc | Send Individually

Subject	

File:

Content

Module 2 Establishing Business Relations

模块 2 建立业务关系

Learning Goals

❖ Know about the key points of writing emails to potential clients in the hope of establishing business relations.
❖ Get familiar with words, expressions and sentence patterns useful for writing to establish business relations.
❖ Be able to write effective sales emails and follow-up emails to establish business relations.

Lead-in

Situation: You're a salesperson. Now your boss asks you to develop business relations in the South-American market. You understand that you may write emails to potential clients to establish business relations with them.

Questions:

1. What would you do before writing to potential clients?
2. What would you mention in the emails to attract replies from potential clients?
3. If you don't receive any reply long after sending the first email, how would you write to follow up?

Task 1 Writing a Sales Email

No customer, no business. To open up or expand a market and promote sales, companies need to establish business relations with new customers. Writing sales emails is one of the cheapest and the most effective ways. A sales email is an email written with the aim of publicizing and ultimately selling a product or a service to potential clients. It is a type of business email for generating business, and also a form of advertising.

Section 1 Guidelines

1. Preparations before writing a sale email

(1) Find out a way to contact potential clients

To open up a new market or expand business activities in an existing market, obtaining information about potential clients is an important step. Traditional information channels include organizations or offices such as the Commercial Counselor's Office（商务参赞处）and Chamber of Commerce（商会）, trade fairs & exhibitions, advertisements, sales agents abroad or old clients or friends.

Nowadays, we frequently search for potential clients on the Internet by using search engines or some B2B websites.

Some contact information may be obtained by SNS (Social Networking Services), that is, by employing social media websites and Apps.

(2) Analyze potential clients

Research potential clients. Know something about the business positioning（定位）of the company and its product, its size and its market, etc. Identify main selling points and benefits of our products which may best suit potential clients.

After taking the above steps, we may proceed to write a sale email to express our hope for establishing business relations.

2. Important components of a sales email

Since a sales email is a form of advertising and is meant for generating business, it often follows the AIDA principle: **attention, interest, desire and action.** We try to get attention or curiosity of potential clients, arouse their interest, mention the benefits of products or services to inspire the desire of them to buy the products or services, and finally encourage them to take action such as replying to our email or placing an inquiry.

Generally speaking, the following components are important for a sales email.

- a subject
- the source of information（信息来源）
- a brief company introduction
- a product/service introduction
- a closing to attract the reply

(1) Write a subject of the sales email

A lot of recipients report an email as spam based on the subject alone. Hence, writing a good subject will help reduce the chance of our sales email being reported as spam. In addition, since a sales email is a way of advertising and marketing, a good subject serves to draw the clients to read the email.

- Re: we are the manufacturer of lights (×)
- Re: need cooperation (×)

The above subjects are undesirable, for they contain little information that may impress the recipients or motivate them to read the email. A subject may include some of the following contents.

- one of our key products
- one of new/unique model/design
- one important selling point of our products
- one of our biggest clients
- one important advantage of our company
- the discount or the special price we offer now
- our company's name

Suppose the name of our company is **DEF Co., Ltd.** We specialize in **solar light**, and our biggest client is **ITALY AIRPORT**. We may write the subject in the following ways.

- Re: Good Quality Solar Light from DEF of China.
- Re: Solar Light/Italy Airport's Supplier/DEF Co., Ltd.
- Re: Solar Light-UNIQUE MODEL!!!/Italy Airport's Supplier.

(2) Mention the source of information

The source of information is often mentioned at the beginning of the sales email because it's helpful to convince our clients that we are a well-established company and a reliable supplier in the business circle.

Suppose we met our potential customer at the Dental Show and write a sales email after the show, you may begin the email with:

- *Glad to meet you at the DENTAL SHOW!*

In this case, we may even use capital letters to draw attention of potential clients. Hopefully, the recipients may spend more time reading the email instead of taking it as spam.

However, it is advisable to understate the information channel if we just get the email address of potential clients by searching the Internet. In this case, we may say: "Glad to know that you are…". For example:

- *Glad to know that you are a leading wholesaler of bikes in Europe.*
- *Glad to learn that you are looking for suppliers of leather bags.*

(3) Introduce the company

In a sales email, we should write our company introduction in a very concise way, covering only the strengths of our company, such as:

- business scope, history, experience, etc.
- production capacity
- trade capacity(business performance)
- distinguished clients
- R&D(Research and Development) capacity
- quality control process

(4) Introduce new/unique/featured products

Products are the lifeline for a company in international trade. An impressive product introduction is the most important part of a sales email.

① Emphasize benefits, new/unique/featured products

It's important to build connections between our products/services and their needs, allowing them to know the benefits offered by our products/services.

② Convince potential clients with proof

To make our sales email convincing, list some figures (e.g., sales figures and annual revenue), facts (e.g., R&D capacity, number of production lines, quality control process, certifications, trademarks, patents), customer feedback, etc.

We should avoid generalizations (泛泛而谈) and cliches (陈词滥调) such as "good quality" "reasonable price" "excellent service". Try to use specific expressions to convince potential clients. For example:

- save up to 15% cost
- improve productivity by 10%
- have a production capacity of 210 000 pcs/month

Besides, the important information may be highlighted with **bold font**.

(5) Urge action and attract reply

At the end of the email, we may invite the recipient to visit our company or factory, or offer a product catalogue, videos, discounts or samples to attract their attention. For that purpose, it's advisable to use "Please …" "Would you please …?" to urge action or ask a question to attract a reply.

Compare the following sentences:

- We will send you samples for free if you wish to have samples for evaluation.
- Would you like to have our FREE SAMPLES for evaluation?
- Please reply "Yes" to this email if you'd like to have our FREE SAMPLES.

The second one and the third one are better because they make the email easier for the recipient to respond. Most desirably, we make our call-to-action crystal-clear (清楚明白) and hard to resist.

Section 2 Samples

Sample 1

To: fred_picker@detek.com
From: alisa_chen@weichi.com
Subject: Patented Mountain Bikes & Road Cars/Supplier of G&K/10 Years' Experience[1]

Dear Mr. Picker[2],

Glad to know from alibaba.com that you are a leading wholesaler of bikes in Europe.[3]

This is Alisa from Weichi Co., Ltd., a well-established **mountain bike and road car manufacturer** in Guangzhou, China.[4] We have more than **10 years' experience** in the manufacturing industry and have been a supplier **of G&K** for 3 years, helping it expand its middle-end market in Europe.[5]

If purchasing from us, you will have:
—an exclusive distribution right in your market;
—a stable market, as we provide CE certified quality products with trendy new designs at competitive prices;
—professional maintenance and after-sales services, as we have a pool of experienced engineers.

With a talented R&D team of more than 30 people, we can design and release new models every month, and many of our bikes and scooters are patented. We also offer OEM and ODM services, as well as customization services for packaging and logo.[6]

Welcome to visit our factory or test our samples. Please reply "Yes" if you would like to have our catalogues and product videos.[7]

Best regards,

Alisa Chen
Sales Representative
Weichi Co., Ltd.

📞 +8620 36×××× | +86158508×××××
✉ alisachen@weichi.com
🌐 www.weichi.com

Comments

1. 在电子邮件的主题中,用词组的形式列出公司产品的主要优势、特点、折扣等,表明公司实力,可以吸引客户打开邮件并阅读;词组之间用斜杠或逗号隔开,也可以整合成短语或短句。

2. 尽可能找出收件人姓名,这样可使称呼更亲切,尽量不要用"Dear Sir/Madam"。

3. 陈述信息来源(如组织机构、交易会、展览会、广告、国外代理商、客户或朋友、跨境电商平台或网站),以佐证公司的可靠性及实力。

4. 写出写信人名字、公司的简称、所在省或市和/或其在中国的地理位置,如"in Guangzhou, China""in East China's Zhejiang Province""in South China's Guangdong Province" "in Ningbo, a City in East China"等。

5. 用几句话简要介绍公司,列出关键信息以及能体现公司优势的要点,如公司的历史、业务范围、主要产品、生产能力、销售业绩、主要市场、研发能力和重要客户等。

6. 简明列出与我方公司合作可带给客户的收益,介绍公司的新产品或特色产品、独家的设计、样式或型号以及产品质量、销售情况、所获的质量认证、客户满意度、可提供的特色服务。这些内容可用项目编号的形式一一列出,重要信息用粗体。

7. 结尾可邀请客户验厂,提出可以提供产品目录、产品视频、折扣或免费样品等,以吸引收件人的注意;在本封邮件中,发件人提出收件人只需简单回复"Yes"即可获得我方的产品目录和视频,意在提升邮件回复率。

Core Vocabulary

leading	*adj.* 领先的
wholesaler	*n.* 批发商
release	*v./n.* 公布;发布
R&D(Research and Development)	研发
manufacturer	*n.* 生产商、制造商
distribution	*n.* 分销,经销
maintenance	*n.* 维护,维修
customization	*n.* 定制
catalogue (catalog)	*n.* 产品目录

> OEM(Original Equipment Manufacturer)原始设备制造商,指由委托方设计或制定规格,由被委托方生产产品。
>
> ODM(Original Design Manufacturer)原始设计制造商,指制造方根据委托方要求,提供从研发、设计到生产、维护的全部服务,即生产方有设计能力,从设计到生产都由生产方自行完成。

Extended Vocabulary

middle-end market	中端市场
exclusive	*adj.* 专有的,独有的
exclusive distribution right	独家经销权

Sample 2

To: a-crajicek@ede.com
From: jack-li@fiberglassproducer.com
Subject: Supplier of SDM & STAR MATS/15% Discount

Dear Mr. Crajicek,

Glad to know that you are a leading wholesaler of fiberglass.

This is Jack from Huirong Co., Ltd. in Tianjin, a city in North China. We have been engaged in exporting **fiberglass products** for **7 years**, supplying mat with superior quality and reasonable prices.

We have passed **ISO 9001** and all our products are **CE certified**. Our distinguished clients including **SDM** and **STAR MATS** are quite satisfied with our products.

If you purchase from us, you will have the following benefits:
　　—**saving up to 10% cost** compared with products of the same kind.
　　—**on-time delivery**, as we have a production capacity of up to 210 000 pcs/month.

We would like to extend a special offer for your first sample order, with a **15% discount** (for the first container).

Please let us know if you'd like to have our **FREE SAMPLES**.

Thanks & best regards,

Jack Li
Huirong Co., Ltd
Skype: jackli4521
―――――――――――――
📞 +86 15820 ×××××
✉ jack-li@fiberglassproducer.com

Core Vocabulary

be engaged in	从事(某一业务)
certify	认证
distinguished	*adj.* 重要的,尊贵的
production capacity	产能

container	*n.* 集装箱

Extended Vocabulary

fibreglass	*n.* 玻璃纤维,玻璃丝
mat	*n.* 垫子

Sample 3

To: c-drabarangsi@topedt.com
From: rockychen@andusafety.com
Subject: Vendor of Wal-Mart/13 Years' Experience/Manufacturer

Dear Ms. Drabarangs,

Glad to learn you're in the market for PPE products.

We, **Andu Safety**, are one of the major manufacturers and suppliers of personal protective equipment in Guangzhou, China. With 250 workers, 30 000 m² dust-free workshop and 13 years' experience, we have been **a vendor of Wal-Mart for 4 years** and have established stable relations with our global clients.

Our main products cover most PPE industry products and our featured products are all types of safety vests, which are **ISO & CE certified**.

Please tell us if you'd like to have our price list and samples.

Best regards,

Rocky
Andu Safety
skype: rocky12345

☎ +86 158xxxxxxxx
✉ rocky1@andusafety.com
🌐 www.andusafety.com

Core Vocabulary

vendor	*n.* 卖主,供应商
in the market for	求购
workshop	*n.* 车间

Extended Vocabulary

PPE (personal protective equipment)	个人防护用品
coverall	*n.* 罩衣
vest	*n.* 马甲

Sample 4

To: dantini_amin@gentpace.com
From: jessie_wang@kattejewelry.com
Subject: Top Jewelry OEM/ODM Manufacturer/MOQ: 50pcs

Hi Mr. Dantini,

This is Jessie from **KATTE JEWELRY COMPANY**, one of the top professional jewelry **OEM/ODM manufacturers** in South China, supplying and designing **925 silver jewelry** and **fashion jewelry in brass and alloy**, which are of fashionable designs and made of safe materials.

For the trial order, we accept a MOQ of only 50 pieces.

FREE SAMPLES are offered for quality test.

Any questions, please contact me directly.

Best regards,
Jessie Wang
Sales Assistant
KATTE JEWELRY COMPANY

📞 86-755-86028xxx | Mobile:86-13588877xxx
✉ jessiewang@katteXXXX.com
📍 Longhua, Shenzhen, China.

Comments
若在邮件正文中插入图片,图片尺寸一般设置为 600~800px。若插入多张图片,注意需要统一尺寸。

Core Vocabulary

MOQ (minimum order quantity)	最小订单量,起订量
jewelry	n. 珠宝,首饰
trial order	试购,试订单

Extended Vocabulary

brass	n. 黄铜
alloy	n. 合金

Section 3 Core Phrases and Sentence Patterns

1. State the source of information

- glad to know/learn(from…)that…

  Glad to know from alibaba.com that you are an importer of mechanical products.

  Glad to learn that you are looking for suppliers of leather bags.

- learn from…

  We learn from alibaba.com that you are looking for suppliers of leather bags.

  We learn from amazon.com that you are experienced in the import of engineering equipment.

- in the market for

  Glad to know that you are in the market for electric saws.

  We are glad to learn that you are in the market for car tools.

2. Introduce the company

(1) Mention business scope & history

- We are one of the leading manufacturers of various kinds of leather bags in China, having been engaged in this line since 1997.
- We are a leading supplier of electric motors in a wide range of specifications.
- We have been specialized in exporting heavy trucks and related parts and components for 10 years.
- We have been a precision gear (高精度齿轮) manufacturer since 2001.

(2) Mention production capacity, business performance and R&D capacity

- Our production capacity of welding machine (焊接机) reaches 60 000 sets per year.
- Our gross sales reached USD 1 billion last year.
- Our annual revenue is around USD 50 million.
- We have a professional R&D team of over 30 senior engineers.

(3) Mention distinguished clients, pilot projects (样板工程)

- Coca-Cola, Nestle, Disney and Pepsi are among our distinguished clients.
- We have been a vendor of Wal-Mart since 2005.
- Our LED lights were used at the 2012 Summer Olympic Games.

Core Vocabulary

line	n. 行业；业务范围
specification	n. 规格
be specialized in	专注于
gross sales	总销售额
annual revenue	年营业额

3. Introduce the products

(1) Emphasize benefits to the client
- You will have the following benefits:
  —saving up to 15% cost
  —on-time delivery, as we have a production capacity of 210 000 pcs/month
- Our training application will help you reduce recruiting (招聘) and training cost.

(2) Mention new/unique/featured products, designs, styles or models
- Up to 5 new smartphone accessories are released monthly.
- We supply LED TV and video walls with the latest digital technology.

(3) Highlight quality of our products
- Our smartwatches are CE, ROHS and FCC certified.
- The toys meet CE, ASTM and CPSIA standards.
- Our notebook computer features a long battery time, with power consumption 5% lower than products of the same kind.

(4) Mention services we can provide
- We provide OEM & ODM services for racing car toys.
- Customization service is provided for packaging.
- Our experienced engineers will provide professional maintenance and after-sales services.
- A full 12-year warranty is provided for the solar panel (太阳电池板).
- All products come with our 60-day money-back guarantee.

Core Vocabulary

accessory	n. 配件，配饰
latest	adj. 最新的
digital technology	数字技术
meet … standards	达到……标准
feature	n. 特色，特点
	v. 以……为主要特点
power consumption	耗电量
warranty	n. 保修
guarantee	n. 担保

---

warranty 和 guarantee 的区别

warranty: a written guarantee promising to repair or replace an article if necessary within a specified period，即生产厂家或卖家出具的产品保修证书，即在某一期限内如果所卖出的产品出了质量问题，生产厂家或卖家负责修理、零件更换乃至退货或更换整个产品。

guarantee: a formal assurance that certain conditions will be fulfilled, especially that a product will be of a specified quality，即机构或个人为产品所承诺的质量水平所签署的责任担保证书，以保证商业交往的另一方不受损失，如商品的质量保证书等。

4. Urge action and attract reply

Would you like to…?

- Would you like to have our FREE SAMPLE for evaluation?

For…, please…

- For a free consultation about our application, please reply to this email.
- For more information, please reply "OK".

If…, please…

- If you'd like to have our FREE SAMPLES, please reply "Yes" to this email.

Task 2 Writing to Follow-up

If we don't receive any reply long after sending the initial sales email, what shall we do?

The answer is to follow up. Following up is an important step in our efforts to establish business relations with potential clients.

Section 1 Guidelines

In the opening part of a follow-up email, we draw the recipient's attention by mentioning our previous email, such as "In my email of October 20, I…". If we have met the client, we should remind him/her by writing "We met at…".

What's more important, we may catch the attention of the recipient by:
- best sellers
- a new product launched
- a product promotion with a special offer

We may also invite the recipient to visit our company or factory in the follow-up email.

After a trade fair, we may send an email to potential clients who visited our booth. It's better to take a photo with the potential clients when they are at our booth and attach the photo to the email. It not only shows our friendliness but also reminds the clients of their visit to our booth.

Section 2 Samples

Sample 1 follow up after a sales email

Subject: Re: Patented Mountain Bikes & Road Cars from Weichi/Client of G&K/ 10 Years' Experience[1]
Dear Mr. Picker,

Me again, Alisa from Weichi. Did you receive my email of October 15?[2]

I'd like to recommend one of our **BEST SELLERS** to you. It is well-received in the European market and we have repeated orders from our clients. Would you like to have a try in your state?[3]

Attached are the photos and specifications. FREE samples of important components used in our bikes will be sent to you upon request.[4]

Kind regards,
Alisa

📎 File (1)

Attachment

Best sellers of Weichi.pdf (604.63K)
Download Preview Add to Favorites Save to ▾

Comments

1. 可选择回复前一封客户开发邮件(选择"全部回复"),这样显示"Re:"字样,让客户知道我们之前写过邮件,同时前一封邮件的内容就能显示在邮件下方。也可以另拟标题,突出本次跟进邮件的主要内容。

2. 提醒客户我们之前写过邮件。

3. 推荐热销产品或促销产品,以吸引收件人的注意,或者邀请收件人在贸易展览会上参观展位、参观公司或工厂等。

4. 通过提出可提供免费样品、折扣或可根据客户具体要求进行报价等,吸引收件人回复邮件。

Core Vocabulary

recommend	*v.* 推荐
well-received	*adj.* 反响很好的,受到欢迎的
repeated order	续订单

Sample 2 the second follow-up email

To: fred_picker@detek.com
From: alisa_chen@weichi.com
Subject: Re: New Design of Mountain Bikes from Weichi[1]

Dear Mr. Picker,

Me again, Alisa from Weichi.

In my email of October 20, I recommend a hot sale item. Are you interested in it?

We also develop a new design for mountain bikes recently. We're glad to tell you that a big order for the new mountain bike was just placed by a client from South America.

Attached is the photo of the new design. Any advice on it?[2]

Best regards,
Alisa

Comments

1. 在邮件主题中，用"新设计"这个词来吸引潜在客户。
2. 为公司新设计的产品寻求潜在客户的意见。如果客户打开图片查看并发来一些改进意见，我们就有了进一步跟进的理由。

Sample 3 invite a client to attend a trade fair

To: fred_picker@detek.com
From: alisa_chen@weichi.com
Subject: Re: Canton Fair Invitation from Weichi, October 31 to November 4, Guangzhou, China[1]

Hi Mr. Picker,

Good day.

It's me, Alisa from Weichi.

Will you attend the coming Canton Fair from October 31 to November 4, 2019? If yes, welcome to visit our booth.

- Booth No.: 16.2H37
- Company Name: Weichi Co., Ltd.
- Date: Phase 3, October 31 to November 4, 2019[2]

Attached is an invitation letter from us.

Look forward to meeting you. If you need any help or have any questions, please contact me.

Alisa

Comments

1. 在邮件主题里写出所有重要信息：写信目的（邀请参加中国进出口商品交易会）、时间及地点、邀请方公司名称。即使收件人没有打开邮件，重要信息也一目了然。另外，我方公司的名字也应明确写出来，即使收件人没有打开邮件，只要收件人扫了一眼邮件主题，推广公司的目的也达成了一部分。

2. 在正文写出所有收件人参加展会所需的信息，并附上邀请函（邀请函里列出更详细信息并为潜在客户提供更多指引）。

Core Vocabulary

Canton Fair　　　中国进出口商品交易会
booth　　　　　　n. 展位
phase　　　　　　n. 阶段，时期

Sample 4　follow up after the trade fair

To: fred_picker@detek.com
From: alisa_chen@weichi.com
Subject: Customized Mountain Bikes (Alisa from Weichi/We Met Today)[1]

Hi Mr. Picker,

Nice evening.

This is Alisa from Weichi. We met today. Please check our photo on the booth.[2]

About the mountain bikes that you're interested in, please find the attached datasheet and pictures.

Price may differ slightly for different specifications and sizes of orders.

For more requirements, please inform or visit us.

Sincerely,
Alisa

Comments

1. 潜在客户白天参观了我们的展位后，我们当天晚上发出了跟进邮件。在邮件主题写明与客户在展会上见过，以唤起客户的记忆。

2. 客户一天可能去了好多个展位参观，附上展会中与收件人的合影，有助于唤起客户的记忆。

Core Vocabulary

datasheet　　*n.* 数据表

inform　　　*v.* 告知

Section 3　Core Phrases and Sentence Patterns

1. **I'd like to recommend**…
- I'd like to recommend one of our **BEST SELLERS** to you.
- I'd like to recommend our unique model.

2. **Attached is (are)**…
- Attached are the photos and specifications.
- Attached is our latest catalogue.

3. **…will be sent upon request.**
- Free samples will be sent to you upon request.
- A detailed quotation sheet will be sent to you upon request.

Tips

客户开发邮件是一种营销邮件，因此要非常注重其营销功能。它比其他类型的函电更强调简洁性，一般只在邮件里写入能够有助于推销本公司产品或服务的内容，其他内容尽量不要放。例如，下述这封客户开发邮件便有很多地方可以删减或修改。

Dear Katherine:

Thanks for taking the time to read my Email. I know you're very busy.

This is Catty from DEF Co., Ltd. in Shenzhen. (可再加上一两句介绍公司的话) Very glad to write to you here! It's my pleasure to be in service with you if possible!

I can give you the CSM at a very competitive price and higher quality. (可再加上两三句介绍产品的话) If you need more information, please go to our website: www.fiberglassproducer.com.

I wonder if you need this product; if you are interested, please kindly return this mail. Maybe now you have a regular business partner. If so, please leave my message in your email box, for maybe someday it will be useful.

Welcome to visit our company if you have time! We'll arrange the car to pick you up from the airport. It's convenient to visit our company, It's just 15 kilometers from the airport.

Yours sincerely,
Catty

DEF Co.,Ltd
Tel：×××
Fax：×××
Mail：×××
Website：www.fiberglassproducer.com

  邮件要注意选择送达时间,需留意时差以及对方上班时间及节假日安排。例如,欧美星期六、星期天不上班,阿拉伯和穆斯林国家星期五、星期六不上班。

  跟进潜在客户切忌过于频繁,令人厌烦,最重要的是找准客户的潜在需求。若客户一直没有回应,可一个月或两个月跟进一次,重点是让客户记住自己,知道己方公司主要做什么产品,主要优势是什么。

  发送客户开发邮件,最担心被判定为垃圾邮件。一般来说,如下情况被判定为垃圾邮件的概率比较高。

  (1) 未经收件人允许的一段时间内,发送频率过快,内容重复度过高。

  (2) 对方未订阅但发件人发送附件。

  (3) 邮件中含有垃圾邮件高频词。

因此,第一封开发信尽量不要使用附件(attachment),如果带有附件,一般不超过 2M。

以下为与销售有关的垃圾邮件高频词。如果开发信被退回,可尝试修改,去掉这些高频词。

free, discount, opportunity, win, winner, cheap, deal, price, rate, profit, save, merchant, stock, act now, call now, subscribe now, opportunity, compare, check, cash, bonus, credit, buy direct, get paid, order now, specializing, specialized, offer, please read, don't delete, special promotion.

Communication Laboratory

I. Fill in each of the following blanks with a proper word/words given in the box. Change the form where necessary.

reach	reasonable	sell well	professional
leading	release	warranty	recommend

1. FYI (for your information), the PPE products _____ in Europe.

2. We are a _____ manufacturer of top-class digital items, such as tablet PCs, mobile phones and accessories. We have a _____ R&D team and are able to _____ at least 5 new models monthly.

3. We are devoted to developing, producing and selling top-class digital items at _____ prices.

4. Our production capacity _____ 30 000 sets monthly.

5. I would like to _____ our latest item No. CA77T.

6. As a major auto manufacturer, we keep on improving our after-sale services, including extending the _____ period.

II. Translate the following sentences into English.

1. 很高兴从贵公司网站上了解到贵公司是机器人玩具的主要经销商(dealer)之一。

2. 我公司是广东省领先的体育用品生产商,从 2003 年起从事该行业。

3. 我公司的月产能是 200 万台户外太阳能(solar)LED 灯。

4. 我公司的大客户有 LLA、CDH 等。

5. 我们的汽车零部件获得 ISO 9001 认证。
_____

6. 我公司发布了最新款的 ICEM 2018。
_____

7. 与市面上的同类产品相比，我公司的包装机可节省多达 10% 的用电。
_____

8. 我公司的无人机（drone）享受 10 年保修服务。
_____

9. 我公司可提供定制服务，以满足贵公司的具体需求。
_____

10. 我想向您推荐我司最新的智能腕带（smart wristband）。
_____

III. Write a sales email based on the situation given.

1. 我公司的名字为 KATT Co., Ltd.，是汽车配件的生产商和出口商，成立于 1998 年，主要从事机电产品的研发，如电动马达（electric motor）和雨刮器（windscreen wiper）。我们的产品在国内外广受欢迎，已获得 QS、ISO 9001、CE 和 ROHS 认证。我们的大客户有 Auto Zone 和 Advanced Auto Parts 等，待开发客户为印度机电产品进口商。

Subject: _____

Content:

Module 2　Establishing Business Relations
模块 2　建立业务关系

2. Please visit alibaba.com and find out a company you're interested in. Suppose you're the salesperson of this company, please draft a sales email to promote products to a company in Colombia (contact person: Carlos Morales Garcia).

Subject:

Content:

3. Suppose you don't receive reply after sending the email written above. Please write an email to follow up.

Subject:

Content:

Module 3 Inquiries

模块 3 询盘

Learning Goals

- Get familiar with different types of inquiries.
- Know about how to analyze an inquiry and the key points for replying to an inquiry.
- Be able to write an inquiry email to potential suppliers.
- Be able to reply to an inquiry.

Lead-in

Situation 1: You are a purchaser of a Chinese company. Now you are preparing to purchase from foreign companies to complete a sourcing project.

Question: How would you write to potential suppliers to inquire about the product you want to buy?

Situation 2: You are a salesperson. Now you receive an inquiry from a South-American company. It is the first time you receive an inquiry from this company.

Questions:

1. What are you supposed to do after receiving the inquiry?
2. What information shall be included in your reply to the inquiry?

Task 1 Writing an Inquiry

Inquiry (or "enquiry") is a request from a buyer to a seller for sales information such as the availability or supply of goods, price terms and discount, delivery date, terms of payment and shipment, etc.

A buyer often sends inquiries to many suppliers at the same time. The purpose of sending inquiries to different suppliers is to ensure that the buyer has a full picture of the product/service. The buyer may make comparisons between the terms and conditions of the incoming offers and decide which offer is the most favourable and choose the most suitable supplier. Buyers often make inquires before the purchasing season of their company or factory. However, a businessperson may send inquires whenever he/she wants some sales information.

Section 1　Guidelines

1. Preparations before writing an inquiry

(1) Find out the right supplier

It is important to find a reliable supplier to ensure we are supplied with what we need. Analyze the potential supplier to see if it's the right one before we actually send an inquiry.

(2) Determine the purpose and type of the inquiry to be sent

Are we just researching the market to prepare for the coming buying season? Are we looking for a specific product? The purpose will determine the type of inquiry to be sent.

Generally speaking, inquiries can be classified into the following types.

① General inquiry（一般询价）. An inquiry that asks for general information, such as catalogues, price lists, samples, pictures, etc. Often, it shows interest in a general product type without specifically mentioning the exact product or other requirements.

When a buyer makes a general inquiry, he/she often aims at collecting supplier information such as price, delivery time, supply capability, etc., for comparison.

② Specific inquiry（具体询价）. An inquiry that inquires about a specific product. It mentions the name of the commodity, specification, quantity, unit price, date of shipment, payment terms, packing, etc.

If a buyer is able to give specific requirements when making an inquiry, it often means that he/she is ready to buy.

It is practical to keep in mind some helpful notes for writing an inquiry email.

① Make your needs clear. We need to make sure the recipient fully understand our request. By that, they can provide a proper response. Let them know which and how much information we look for. Try using a numbered list so they can easily check if they have satisfied our needs.

② Set a deadline. For things to operate smoothly, we'd better set a deadline. Instead of just letting it be, mentioning an expected deadline can create reminders for the recipient.

2. Structure of an inquiry email

An inquiry email generally contains the following components.

(1) Subject

(2) Opening

- stating the source of information
- briefly introducing the buyer's company(if it's the first inquiry sent to the supplier)
- stating the purpose of writing

(3) Body
- asking for information: a catalogue, a price list, a detailed quotation, etc.
- indicating details of the requirement

(4) Closing
- asking for a reply from the potential supplier
- indicating the urgency of the inquiry, if necessary
- giving a deadline (期限) if necessary

When requesting a lot of detailed information, it is suggested that the inquiry be written in bullet points(使用编号一一列出). This avoids missing any important details.

Section 2 Samples

Sample 1 a specific inquiry

Subject: Inquiry for Car DVD Player[1]

Dear Sir/Madam,

We come to know at the Canton Fair that you are a supplier of electronic products in Germany.[2] We are a large retailer of electronic products in South China's Guangdong Province and we are looking for a manufacturer who could supply us with a wide range of car audio and video products.[3]

Please quote the following item:

Name: Car DVD player
Size: 10.1 inch
Specification: Bluetooth-Enabled, with built-in GPS
Quantity: 1 000 sets
Shipment: CIF Guangzhou

Please send us your specific quotation, indicating delivery terms and all other relevant information.[4]

Since this is an urgent purchase, please kindly reply by October 20, 2020.[5]

Thanks and best regards,

Huang Yilian
ABC Electronics Co., Ltd.

Comments
1. 在"主题"处写明写信人想要询盘的产品名称。
2. 说明信息来源,佐证写信人公司的资质及可靠性。
3. 简短介绍写信人的公司。
4. 写信人希望收信人提供的信息,如报价及报价要求等。
5. 请求收件的答复。如果本询盘为紧急询盘或希望收信人在某一期限前回复,应予以说明。

Core Vocabulary

retailer	n. 零售商
shipment	n. 船运
quotation	n. 报价
indicate	v. 写明;标示
relevant	adj. 相关的
purchase	n./v. 采购

Extended Vocabulary

bluetooth-enabled	有蓝牙功能的
built-in GPS	内置 GPS(global positioning system)

Sample 2 a specific inquiry

Subject: Inquire about the Availability of Truck Tire[1]

Dear Mr. Johns,

We are an importer of industrial products to China and we are interested in your truck tire.[2]

Please let me know whether you're able to supply the D333 truck tire. If yes, please send us your latest catalogue with a price list.[3]

Do you give discounts or special offers for quantity orders? Please kindly reply ASAP.[4]

Regards,
(Miss)Chen Lihui
Purchaser
Amoy International Ltd.

Comments

1. 主题写明写信人想要询问某样产品是否有货。
2. 简要提及写信人的公司性质以及写信目的。
3. 写明希望收信人提供的资料。
4. 请求收信人的答复,这里特别说明想了解卖方是否提供大单折扣或优惠价。

Core Vocabulary

availability	n. 可用性,可得性
inquire about the availability	询问某种产品是否可供货
ASAP (as soon as possible)	尽快

Sample 3   a general inquiry

Subject: Looking for Outdoor Equipment[1]

Dear Mr. Lacona,

We learn from Alibaba.com that you are supplying outdoor equipment. We are a leading wholesaler in Sichuan Province, China, and we wish to find out more information about your products.[2]

Please give us your price list and catalogue, stating your MOQ, delivery time and terms of payment, etc.[3]

Look forward to your early reply.[4]

Sincerely,
(Mr) Chen Bo
Purchasing Manager
Mino Trading Co.,Ltd.

Comments

1. 本询盘为一般询盘,主题写明写信人求购某种产品。
2. 写明信息来源、公司概况以及写信目的。
3. 写明希望收信人提供的资料及信息。
4. 请求收件人答复。

Section 3　Core Phrases and Sentence Patterns

1. Write the subject of the inquiry

The subject can be written in the following ways.

- Inquiring about… (e. g. the availability of laptops)
- Inquiry for… (e. g. silver needle earrings)
- Request for… (catalogues)
- Looking for… (e. g. industrial materials)

2. State the source of information; state the purpose of writing; briefly introduce the writer's company (if it's the first inquiry sent to the supplier)

- We have come to know that you are a distributor of indoor advertising TV in Germany. We specialize in the import of electronic products to China and would like to know if you can give us a quotation.
- We learn from the Hong Kong Fair that you are a leading manufacturer of balance scooters in the U. S. We are an importer in China and are interested in your scooters.
- We are in the market for high capacity power bank and would like to inquire about its availability in your factory.
- We are interested in your cotton Table-Cloth Art. No. 65 and 76.

3. Ask for information: a catalogue, a price list or a quotation, etc.

- Please kindly send us your electronic catalogue and price list.
- Please get back to me with specific quotes, delivery terms and all other relevant information.
- Would you please quote us a price for two-wheel smart balance scooters?
- Please quote us the lowest CIF Seattle prices for silver needle earrings.
- We wish to have your lowest offer for storage racks (存放架).
- Please make a quotation for touch-screen indoor advertising TV on FOB Guangzhou basis.
- We'd like to have your lowest CIF Sydney offer for kids' soccer jerseys.
- Please let us know what quantities you can supply from stock.
- Please let me know whether you could offer samples free of charge.

4. Ask for a reply; give a deadline

- I look forward to receiving your early reply.
- This is an urgent purchase. Please reply ASAP.
- Please reply by October 20, 2020.

Task 2 Replying to Inquiries

A sale often begins with an inquiry from a potential customer. Unfortunately, sellers too often respond to these inquiries without much thought, which can result in problems down the road, particularly if this inquiry represents a potential export sale.

A buyer often sends inquiries to many potential suppliers at the same time. For a seller, receiving inquiries means potential business but very likely he/she is also facing many competitors. The seller should take great care to make the reply more conducive to business.

Section 1 Guidelines

1. Compass

After receiving an inquiry, we may take the following steps.

(1) Have a quick analysis of the inquiry

A brief analysis of the inquiry may help us make a reply that better suit the needs of the client, thereby improving the outcome of our export sale.

① Determine the type of inquiry and priority of replying

In case we receive general inquiries and specific inquiries at the same time, often **specific inquiries are replied to first**. For a seller, receiving a specific and detailed inquiry often means greater business opportunity than receiving a general inquiry.

We may also check whether a deadline is given or whether it is in ungency.

② Identify possible concerns of the inquirer（询盘人）

Try to guess the inquirer's chief concerns: price, quality, delivery time, or R&D capacity.

For the first inquiry, check the background of the inquirer.

Try to answer the following questions.

- Is the inquirer a factory, a wholesaler, a distributor or a retailer? How large is its possible demand?
- What is the possible position of the writer: boss, purchasing manager, purchaser, engineer or secretary?
- How well does the writer know about the product he/she is inquiring for?

(2) Determine how to reply to the inquiry

Based on the result of the analysis we have previously done, we are thus able to determine the focus of our reply.

In addition, when writing to persons in different posts, the focus of our reply may also differ. For example, if we are replying to a secretary, we may try to provide comparative information and highlight selling points of our products; if replying to a purchaser, we may try to show our professionalism and our work efficiency; if replying to an engineer, we shall provide accurate technical and engineering data; and if replying to the boss of a wholesaler or retailer, we need to highlight the sales performance of our products and the values or profits which our products can bring to him/her.

2. Writing structure

Generally speaking, when replying to a general inquiry, the basic writing structure is as follows.

- thank the inquirer（询盘人）for the inquiry;
- provide all information requested, introducing attachments（附件）;
- provide additional information, which is relevant（相关的）or may be helpful to the inquirer;
- briefly introduce our company (if replying to the first inquiry) & selling points of our products;
- express hope for cooperation, motivate the inquirer to make an early reply.

Section 2 Samples

Sample1 reply to a general inquiry

Sample inquiry email

To: tontonsales@163.com
From: Doraraj@Dedocy.com
Subject: Inquiry for Boy's Wear[1]

Dear Sir/Madam,

We are a trading company and a wholesaler of Children's wear in Canada.

We are interested in all your products.[2] Could you please send us more information about your products and your price list?[3]

Best regards,
C. Doraraj
Dedocy Ltd.

Comments

1. 这是一封询盘邮件。

2. 这是一般询盘，没有提及具体的产品需求。在回复这类询盘时，除了提供对方索要的资料之外，还可根据我们对该潜在客户的市场、目标客户等所做的分析，重点推荐适合对方的产品。

3. 回复时，要想到一个可能吸引潜在客户的点，使其有动力回复我方的邮件。

Sample　reply to the above inquiry

To：Doraraj@Dedocy.com
From：linhua111@163.com
Subject：Re：Reply to Inquiry/ Catalogue & Price-list for Quality Boy's Wear at Competitive Price

Dear Doraraj,

Thanks for your inquiry of September 11, 2020.

Attached are our latest catalogue and price list of products that may suit your market. We'd like to recommend Bob's collection. Our customer in the U.S. has placed many repeated orders for them.[1]

We offer a **3% discount** for bulk purchases. Would you tell us your possible order quantity?[2]

We, Tonton, are a professional manufacturer of children's wear in South China's Guangdong Province. By now our products have been exported to 10 countries and regions including America, Australia and Europe.

Waiting for your reply.

Best regards,

LIN Hua
Export Manager
Tonton Sportswear

Wechat: 158266××××× | Mobile:86-158266×××××
Linhua111@163.com
https://tonton1.en.alibaba.com/
Shenzhen, Guangdong Province, P. R. China,

TONTOS Tonton Sportswear Shenzhen Co.,Ltd
Tel: 0086 - 755 - 89361115　　Fax: 0086 - 755 - 89985625

Comments

1. 提供客户需要的资料，重点推荐热销产品，强调该产品在类似市场卖得好。

2. 表明批量购买可提供折扣，从而吸引对方回复。

Core Vocabulary

suit	v. 适合
collection	n.（常为季节性推出的）系列
repeated order	重复订购
bulk purchase	批量购买

Sample 2　reply to a general inquiry

Sample　inquiry email

To：yihao@qq.com
From：Abdul_aziz@addof.com
Subject：Inquiry for Polymer Products

Dear Sir,

I represent an industrial material supplier in the U.S. and we are interested in polymer products.

Please give us your price list and catalogues, indicating your MOQ, delivery time and terms of payment as soon as possible.[1]

Abdul Aziz
Addof Industrial Co., Ltd.

Comments

1. 这是一般询盘，没有提及具体的产品需求，但提到希望供应商提供 best price, MOQ, delivery time and terms of payment 等信息，且希望尽早回复，表明该买家有一定购买意向，同时比较关注价格、最小订货量、交货时间及付款方式。询盘邮件中提到有关 MOQ 的问题，说明采购数量可能不大，或买家比较谨慎，第一次下单并不想买太多。回复时，要突出我方的价格有竞争力，并明确标示 MOQ, delivery time, terms of payment 等。

Sample　reply to above inquiry

To：Abdul_aziz@addof.com
From：billy_liu@qq.com
Subject：Re: Reply to Inquiry/ Best price of Polymer Products with Timely Delivery/ MOQ: 100pcs[1]

Dear Mr. Aziz,

Thanks for your email showing your interest in our industrial materials.

Attached are our product catalogue and price list.

For first orders, we are willing to accept a small quantity (MOQ: 100pcs). We're sure you'll find our product most satisfactory. Our average lead time for small orders is 5 days. As for payment, we generally accept T/T and irrevocable L/C at sight.[2]

Established in 2001, we, YIHAO, are a leading manufacturer of PTFE and other polymer products. With an R&D team of more than 50 people, we can offer state-of-the-art products and customized solutions for a wide range of industrial needs. We have more than 20 production lines and adopt ISO 9002 standards. Our products have been exported to 20 regions such as East Asia, Central Asia, Europe and North America. Our clients include GE, Daewoo, CRRC, etc.[3]

We offer customized services to suit customers' needs.[4] Would you tell us your requirements so that we can send you more information?

Best regards,
Billy Liu
Yihao Industrial Material Co., Ltd.
Skype/Wechat: 13588877766

📞 86-755-860××××× | Mobile:86-135888×××××
✉ Billy_liu@qq.com
📍 Baoan, Shenzhen, China.

Comments

1. 邮件的主题回应了买家的关切(价格是否低？交货能否及时？能否先下个小订单？)客户一目了然。
2. 在邮件正文明确回应对方的关切。
3. 介绍公司时，突出研发能力、定制服务、产品质量、产品销售情况，列出我方的重要客户，让对方了解我方的产能优势。
4. 表明可根据客户的具体需求提供定制服务，以吸引对方的回复。

Core Vocabulary

state-of-the-art	*adj.* 最先进的
customized	*adj.* 定制的
solution	*n.* 解决方案
production line	生产线

adopt	v. 采取
irrevocable L/C at sight	不可撤销的即期信用证

Extended Vocabulary

polymer	聚合物
PTFE	聚四氟乙烯（一种广泛应用的密封材料）
GE	通用电气公司（美国）
Daewoo	大宇（韩国第二大汽车生产企业）
CRRC	中国中车股份有限公司

Section 3　Core Phrases and Sentence Patterns

1. Thank the recipient for the inquiry

（1）Thank you for your inquiry of July 1 for our lightweight luggage（轻便行李箱）.

（2）Thank you for your email of July 1, showing your interest in our emergency kit（急救盒）.

（3）Thanks for your inquiry of July 1 concerning our LED lights.

2. Provide all information requested, and introduce attachments（附件）

（1）We are pleased to attach our latest price list for…（产品名称）you inquire about.

（2）Attached is our catalogue and price-list, showing details of our…（产品名称）.

3. Express hope for cooperation, and motivate the inquirer to make a reply

（1）We look forward to receiving your order/reply soon.

（2）Would you tell me your detailed address so that we can send you some samples for evaluation?

如何写询盘信？如何回复询盘？

1. 采购员如何写询盘信

如果是比较具体的询盘，应明确采购产品信息和报价要求。如果要求工厂报价，需明确产品的具体要求、数量、配置、认证要求、包装、交货方式等，最好使用编号明确每一项，使供应商接到询盘时能够一目了然，从而较为迅速地准确报盘，而且可以检验对应的业务人员是否认真。若询盘要求里写得很清楚的事项，对方还是不停提问，说明对方没有仔细看相关信息。

询盘时，应运用合适的专业术语。一方面可以让供应商消除询盘是虚假询盘的疑虑，另一方面可以让供应商了解清楚采购需求，及时提供合理的报价反馈。

采购新产品时，要对产品做一定的了解，若有不清楚的内容可以直接问潜在供应商，并在后续的询盘中进行明确。若不清楚应该采购哪种产品或原材料，也可以在询盘中加上以下内容。

Please let me know if there are any better options in the same price range.（请告知我相同的价格范围内是否有更好的选择。）

Please get back to me with relevant information or suitable alternatives.（请告知我相关信息或适合的替代产品。）

It will be appreciated if you could also recommend other alternatives that may suit our market.（如果您还可以推荐其他适合我们市场的替代品，我将不胜感激。）

I appreciate it if you could recommend some hot-sell products which may help us expand the market.（如果您能推荐一些热销产品，帮助我们扩大市场，我将不胜感激。）

发送询盘并与供应商沟通过程中，不要以为自己是顾客，就可以在询盘以及后续沟通中忘记外贸函电写作的"礼貌性"原则，用比较傲慢或随意的语气书写询盘。询盘是一种正式的商务文书，也应使用较为正式及礼貌的语气。

2. 外贸业务员如何回复询盘邮件

（1）收到到客户询盘，不要盲目回复。应先了解客户并分析询盘，包括客户公司的资质、信用状况以及我们的产品是否对应客户的需求，再根据分析结果回复邮件。

（2）制订针对性的回复方案。针对客户的关注点有针对性地回复询盘。

（3）收到询盘后尽早回复，一般不要超过 24 小时。如果不能马上提供对方想要的资料，也应先回复邮件告知已收到询盘，可附上公司的简介、推荐热销产品等，例如：

Dear Peter,

This is Nancy from EPOCH. We have specialized in … in Guangdong, China for over 10 years.

I will reply to all your questions in 4 hours, providing you the followings：

 （1）Detailed introduction to our …（产品名称）

 （2）Quotation for ×× × pcs of …（产品名称）

 （3）Introduction of our hot-sale model ×× ×

 （4）Some suggestions to you before you make the purchase

The attachments are our factory and product introduction and video links for your reference.

Best regards,
Nancy

Communication Laboratory

I. Fill in each of the following blanks with a proper word/words given in the box. Change the form where necessary.

retailer	inquire	manufacturer	quotation
suit	shipment	relevant	catalogue
range	evaluation	indicate	purchase

1. We would like to _____ for storage racks.

2. We're planning to buy some children's scooters. Would you please give us a _____?

3. We are a leading _____ of surgical masks (医用口罩). The monthly output of our factory is over 100 million pieces.

4. DC store is a _____ which sells telecommunications components to end-users(终端用户).

5. _____ of the goods can be made one week from the date of order.

6. It is appreciated if you could include all _____ information in your quotation.

7. Would you tell me your detailed address so that we can send you some samples for _____?

8. Attached are our lastest catalogue and price list of products that may _____ your market.

9. Please kindly _____ terms of delivery in your quotation.

10. Please kindly send us your latest electronic _____.

11. We are planning to _____ 1 000 sets of sports equipment in the next buying season.

12. With more than 50 production lines, we supply a wide _____ of quality sports shoes.

II. Translate the following sentences into English.

1. 我公司了解到贵公司是巴西主要的足球用品经销商。

2. 我公司专注于从欧洲进口电子产品，想知道贵公司能否给我们提供如下报价。

3. 我公司正寻求购买电动马达，请按如下规格进行报价。

4. 请发来贵公司的电子目录。

5. 请问贵公司是否可以免费提供样品？

6. 请提供具体报价以及其他相关信息。

7. 请注明贵公司的最早交货时间。

8. 烦请于 2020 年 11 月 2 日之前答复。

9. 感谢贵方于 12 月 2 日发来的关于儿童背包的询盘（Thank you for…）。

10. 随本邮件附上了产品目录，目录里有儿童背包的图片以及详细规格描述。

III. Write an email in English based on the situation given.

1. Writing an inquiry email (please include the subject)

LTK 国际贸易公司，位于四川成都，主要经营国外进口的美容器械（beauty equipment）。现需要向国外厂家购买面部按摩仪（facial massager），由采购员向德国一家生产商发送询盘。

Subject	
Content	

2. Visit alibaba.com to search for a company selling LED lights. Suppose you're the salesperson of this company, please write a reply (include an email subject) to the given inquiry.

> Dear Sir,
>
> We are interested in your LED lights I saw at alibaba.com, and wish to establish business relations with your company.
>
> Please send your catalogues and price list.
>
> Your early reply is appreciated.
>
> Best regards,
> Paul Carlson

Your reply to the above inquiry.

Subject:

Content:

Module 4 Offers

Learning Goals

❖ Know about factors we shall consider before making an offer.
❖ Know the key points of making an offer.
❖ Be able to make an offer.

Lead-in

Situation: You're a salesperson. Now you receive an inquiry from a South-American company. You're considering making an offer to this potential client.

Questions:

1. What factors would you consider before making an offer?
2. What information shall be included in your offer?
3. Could you suggest some points for attention when making an offer to potential clients?

Making an Offer

Section 1 Guidelines

1. Compass

After receiving a specific inquiry, if it is possible to quote a price directly, we may take the following steps.

(1) Determine the type of offer

① Quotation or offer

When replying to a specific inquiry, we often give a quotation or an offer.

In business, a quotation is a document that a vendor or service provider would give to a customer to describe specific goods and services that he/she may provide.

A quotation is not an "offer" in the legal sense. If a quotation is made together with all necessary terms and conditions of sales, it amounts to an offer.

An offer is a promise to supply or buy goods on the terms and conditions stated. It not only quotes the price of the goods the provider wishes to sell or to buy but also indicates all necessary terms of transactions for the buyer's consideration and acceptance. Thus, we should be very careful when making an offer.

② Firm offer(实盘) or non-firm offer(虚盘)

A firm offer is a promise to sell at a stated price and condition within a stated period. It cannot be withdrawn once it has been accepted. A non-firm offer is an offer made without engagement(没有约束力). It is subject to confirmation after being accepted.

(2) Choose an appropriate trade term when quoting a price

The Incoterms or International Commercial Terms(国际贸易术语解释通则), published by the International Chamber of Commerce(ICC), are the standard terms of trade that define the rights and obligations of the parties involved in the trade. It specifies the responsibility of the buyer and the seller by defining the transaction and the cost aspects concerning the transaction and especially related to carriage(运输), custom duties(关税), as well as insurance, etc. For example, Incoterms 2020 include the following trade terms.

① For any mode of transport(适用于任何运输模式)
- EXW—Ex Works(工厂交货)
- FCA—Free Carrier(货交承运人)
- CPT—Carriage Paid To(运费付至)
- CIP—Carriage and Insurance Paid To(运费和保险费付至)
- DPU—Delivered at Place Unloaded(卸货地交货)
- DAP—Delivered At Place(目的地交货)
- DDP—Delivered Duty Paid(完税后交货)

② For sea and inland waterway transport(适用于海运和内河运输模式)
- FAS—Free Alongside Ship(装运港船边交货)
- FOB—Free On Board(装运港船上交货)
- CFR—Cost and Freight(成本加运费)
- CIF—Cost, Insurance and Freight(成本、保险费加运费)

2. Writing structure

In an offer or a quotation, the basic writing structure is as follows.

(1) Thank the inquirer for the inquiry

(2) State details of the offer, including:
- name of commodities, quantity, specifications, price and price terms;
- terms of payment, packing, shipment, lead time, photos;
- whether the offer is a firm offer or a non-firm offer, and/or the validity of the offer;
- additional information if necessary, such as import license requirements, if known;
- additional certifications and statements required by the buyer's country.

(3) Briefly introduce our company (if replying to the first inquiry) and selling points of our products

(4) Express hope for an order, and motivate the inquirer to make an early reply

Section 2 Samples

Sample 1   reply to a specific inquiry

Sample   inquiry

To: rong_jiaping@hongmeng.com
From: adirake_phupoom@yahoo.com
Subject: Inquiring for Rotary Tillers

Dear Sir,

We are a big agricultural equipment company in Thailand.[1]

Now the cultivation season is approaching and farmers need to use rotary tillers.[2] Could you send us a quotation of rotary tillers (working widths 100—200cm, with shaft and clutch) in bulk price, together with details and pictures?[3]

Regards,
(Mr.) Adirake Phupoom

Comments

1. 询盘人介绍自己是销售农业器械的大型贸易公司,但没说明公司名称,可搜索询盘人的姓名,尝试寻找其公司的资料。若找不到该公司的资料,可通过泰国行业网站了解 rotary tiller (旋耕机) 销售数据,估算中型或大型进口商可能购买的数量。

2. 询盘本身未提及是否为紧急购买,也没给出回复期限。但提到"the cultivation season is approaching",可查询泰国的耕种季是什么时候,判断是否为紧急需求。若为紧急需求,我方需确保及时发货,应在报价时备注发货时间;若我方能较早发货,则我方报价会更有竞争力。

3. 没提及具体的订单数量,只提到希望报 bulk price (批发价),要求附上产品细节及图片，且对产品的规格及参数有明确要求，报价时必须报符合询盘人要求的产品。可搜索泰国常用的 rotary tiller 的类型、质量和价格区间，确保我方报价符合对方需求。

Sample reply to the above inquiry

To: adirake_phupoom@yahoo.com
From: rong_jiaping@zeyimachinery.com
Subject: Re: Reply to Inquiry for Rotary Tillers/Short Lead Time/1 Year Warranty[1]

Dear Mr. Adirake Phupoom, [2]

Thanks for your inquiry of February 20, 2020 for our rotary tillers. [3]

We are pleased to quote rotary tillers with shaft and clutch as follows. [4]

Picture	Model	Power /HP	Number of Blades	Weight /kg	Working width /cm	Price /US $
	1GQN-100	18—20	22	180	100	**380**
	1GQN-125	20—25	26	190	125	**430**
	1GQN-140	25—30	30	200	140	**480**
	1GQN-150	25—30	34	210	150	**530**
	1GQN-160	30—40	38	230	160	**580**
	1GQN-180	50—55	42	350	180	**630**
	1GQN-200	55—75	46	370	200	**680**

Please note the above quotation is based on the following trade terms.

- Term of price: FOB Jinan.
- MOQ: **10 sets. 10% discount** for orders of more than 50 sets.
- Lead time: depending on the size of the order, **10 to 15 days** for orders of less than 50 sets. For larger orders, within 45 days.
- Warranty: 1 year.
- Terms of payment: 50% T/T down payment and the balance against B/L copy.

Please note that the above quotation is valid <u>before April 20, 2020</u>.

This rotary tiller is quite popular in the Southeast market. In 2019, we have sold up to US＄50 million worth of equipment including rotary tillers, harrows and ploughs to the Southeast Asian market.[5]

Attached is a detailed quotation sheet with more pictures and additional information. Catalogues of some other hot-sale equipment are also attached for your reference.[6]

We are an experienced manufacturer of agricultural equipment in Shenzhen, South China. With more than 500 engineers, we can supply various kinds of quality agricultural equipment, featuring timely delivery and superior service.[7]

As the cultivation season is approaching, we advise you to order as soon as possible.[8]

Looking forward to your early reply.

Sincerely,

(Mr.) Rong Jiaping
Sales Manager
Zeyi Machinery
Wechat: 13577667777

Wechat: 135776××××× | Mobile: 86-135776×××××
rong_jiaping@zeyimachinery.com
zeyimachinery.com
Yucheng City, Shandong Province, P. R. China.

Comments

1. 回复邮件时，选择用"回复邮件"功能，让对方知道我方是回复对方的询盘，不是广告邮件；要修改对方之前邮件的主题，突出公司或产品的优势，力求在众多回复邮件中脱颖而出。

2. 从之前对方发来的询盘中，我们可以知道对方的姓名，因此不要以 sir or madam 开头，要称呼对方的名字，以表尊重，也让对方知道我们是专门为他做的针对性回复。

3. 感谢对方的询盘，也让对方回忆起之前下过询盘而重视这封邮件。

4. 本封邮件没有选择先介绍自己公司，而是先回复对方的问题。此处，根据客户要的型号和规格，选择适合对方市场质量要求的产品，结合可能的订单量，做一份图文并茂的报价单，插入邮件正文，附上产品图片、规格及价格，标注最小订单量、大单折扣、付款方式、价格术语、报价有效期等。

5. 简要介绍产品，突出产品适合对方市场等卖点。

6. 以附件的形式附上更详细的报价单，可含更多产品图及更多产品信息，并用另一附件推荐适合对方市场的热销产品。

7. 简要介绍我方公司，突出产品质量好、能确保及时交货等优势。

8. 以产品的销售季临近为由，敦促对方尽早下单。

Core Vocabulary

lead time　　　　　　　　　　　　前置时间（从订购到供应商交货所间隔的时间，通常以天或小时计算）

timely	*adj.* 及时的
superior	*adj.* 优越的、高级的、质量卓越的
approach	*v.* 临近

Extended Vocabulary

rotary tiller	旋耕机、旋转式翻土机
fertilizer spreader	施肥机
harrow	耙
seeder	播种机
plough	犁
planter	插秧机

Sample 2   reply to a specific inquiry

Sample   inquiry

To: tontonsales@163.com
From: johnson_smiths@dotgarments.com
Subject: Inquiry for Football Jersey

Dear Sir,

We are a trading company and wholesaler of sportswear in Australia. We would like to import your Bob's Collection football jersey (the 106.248 series) urgently. [1]

Please give me your price list based on CFR Melbourne, indicating your order quantity, payment terms, delivery time, etc. [2]

Thank you.

Johnson

DOT Garment
5036 dr phillips blvd #201, Melbourne, Australia
Tel: 61-407-92×××××
Fax: 61-407-97×××××
Email: bobsingh555@yahoo.com

Comments

1. 这是具体询盘，产品要求很明确，有自我介绍，也提供了各种联系方式，是高质量询盘，同时邮件中明确提及是"紧急"求购，应优先回复。

2. 询盘人提到希望报 best price、payment terms、delivery time 等，说明比较关注产品价格、付款方式及交货时间，不能遗漏这些信息。询盘没有给出具体的订购量，但提到在报价时标注 order quantity。可根据不同订单量做一个阶梯报价，供客户选择。

Sample reply to the above inquiry

To：johnson_smiths@dotgarments.com
From：linhua111@163.com
Subject：Reply to Inquiry/Best Price for Football Jersey/MOQ：50pcs

Dear Johnson，

Thanks for your inquiry of October 15，2020 and your interest in our football jersey. We're glad to enter into a business relation with you.

We quote without engagement the following best prices for Bob's Collection football jersey(the 106.248 series).[1]

Order Quantity	Payment Terms	Lead Time	Unit Price (CFR Melbourne，in US $)
50 pcs (MOQ for a trial order)	T/T	1 day	11/pc
500 pcs	T/T	5 days	9/pc
1 000 pcs	T/T	7 days	7/pc
More than 1 000 pcs	T/T, Irrevocable L/C at sight	9 days	5/pc

Attached is a detailed quotation with pictures and specifications.

As Australia is our strategic market，we have quoted the most competitive prices to help you push sales.[2]

We would also like to recommend the 112 series. They sell well in Europe and can be supplied from stock.[3] A catalogue of this series is also attached.

If working with us，you will be offered the followings.
- competitive price with prompt delivery
- eco-friendly fabric with comfortable and soft hand-feel
- over 1 000 colors and 200 designs，offering customized designs and logos.[4]

With 18 years' experience，more than 200 technical staff members and 20 production lines，we supply a wide range of quality sportswear. So far，we have established stable business relations with clients in North and South America，Europe and other countries and regions.[5]

Would you tell us your order quantity and packaging requirements? [6]

Hope to receive your early reply.

Best regards,

LIN Hua
Export Manager
Tonton Sportswear

Wechat: 158266××××× | Mobile:86-158266×××××
Linhua111@163.com
https://tonton1.en.alibaba.com/
Shenzhen, Guangdong Province, P. R. China,

TONTOS Tonton Sportswear Shenzhen Co.,Ltd
Tel :0086- 755 89361115   Fax :0086- 755 89885625

Comments

1. 根据客户指定的产品系列，按不同订单量做出阶梯报价单，插入邮件正文，列出客户关心的订单量、交货时间、付款方式、价格术语等。此外，quote without engagement 表明这是一个 non-firm offer。

2. 表明我们的报价非常有竞争力。

3. 推荐可能适合客户的其他热销品，供客户参考及选择。这位客户是紧急询盘，很可能非常关心是否能按时交货，因此重点推荐有现货的产品。

4. 以关键词或短语的形式列出我方产品的主要优势或特色。除了提及产品优势，也可提及我方提供的服务，如定制服务等，凸显我方的服务意识，也为产品增加服务附加值。

5. 为了让客户相信我方按时交货的能力，在简要介绍公司时，突出公司的生产能力强、生产线数量多、交货及时等优势。

6. 抛出问题，引导对方回复邮件。

Core Vocabulary

quote without engagement	无约束力的报价
prompt delivery	交货及时
series	*n.* 系列
eco-friendly	*adj.* 环保的
strategic	*adj.* 战略的
fabric	*n.* 面料
supply from stock	库存供应；现货供应
hand-feel	*n.* 手感

Extended Vocabulary

jersey	*n.* 运动衫
polo shirts	*n.* 保罗衫
hoody	*n.* 帽衫，连帽卫衣

Section 3　Core Phrases and Sentence Patterns

1. Make an offer

(1) Please find our quotation for…(产品名称)as follows.

(2) We are pleased to quote you the best price for…(产品名称)as below.

(3) We are pleased to offer the following competitive prices for…(产品名称).

(4) We are pleased to offer our lowest price for…(产品名称)as follows.

(5) We are pleased to quote you without engagement the followings.

2. Provide additional information, which is relevant or may be helpful to the recipient

(1) We offer a 3% discount for bulk purchases.

(2) We'd like to recommend our…(产品名称). Our customer in…(最好是一个与潜在买家的市场类似的国家或地区)has placed many repeated orders for them.

(3) We invite your attention to our other products such as tablecloths and table napkins, details of which you will find in the catalogue.

3. State whether the offer is a firm offer and/or the validity of the offer

(1) The offer is/remains firm/valid/open/good/effective before…(our time).

(2) The offer remains firm/valid/open/good/effective for ONE MONTH.

(3) This offer is subject to final confirmation(以最终的确认为准).

(4) The offer is subject to your reply before…(our time).

(5) We quote without engagement(无约束力)the following.

(6) The quotation is subject to goods being unsold(以货物未售出为条件).

(7) The quotation is subject to prior sale(以先来先买为准).

4. Express hope for cooperation, and motivate the inquirer to place an order

(1) As…(e. g., the Christmas season, the tourist season, the selling season, etc.) is approaching, we advise you to order as soon as possible.

(2) Please reply as soon as possible since we are heavily committed/because we don't have much in stock.

(3) As there are heavy demands for this line of products, we advise you to order as soon as possible.

(4) As the prices are likely to rise soon, we advise you to order without delay.

Task 2

Following up after Making an Offer

What shall we do if we receive no response from the potential client after sending a reply to his/her inquiry? The answer is: follow up.

Our instincts tell us that if someone hasn't replied to our first email they're not interested, and that they're not going to like it if we bother them again. In this case, our instincts are often wrong.

If our first email remains unanswered, there's still some chance that a prospect replies to a follow-up. That means that if we don't send follow-up emails, we will lose a sizable chunk of business.

Section 1　Guidelines

Follow-up emails should be concise. Most importantly, it should offer something of value.

1. Write a good subject

It's important to test different email subject when following up. The subject should be simple, brief and professional.

Don't write:

How do you feel about our price? (×)

What do you think of the quality of our samples? (×)

Instead, write:

Re:Reply to Inquiry/Increase 15% profit with Unique Style Backpack(√)

Re:Reply to Inquiry/Save up to 10% Cost for Quality Backpack, Small MOQ(√)

2. Add value to the follow-up email

The purpose of following up is to secure a transaction. We do our best to provide customers with all conveniences, professional opinions and optimized solutions, to solve problems for potential clients, and to make them profitable so as to achieve a win-win result. Therefore, we should never send a follow-up without demonstrating our worth. Avoid lazy follow-ups. Instead, provide value at each interaction. Make it worthwhile for the client to open, click, and respond.

Section 2　Samples

Sample 1　the first follow-up email

Subject:Re:Reply to Inquiry/ Rotary Tillers with Stable Performance [1]

Dear Mr. Adirake Phupoom,

Good morning!

I just want to follow up on the quotation I sent on February 20 for our rotary tillers. Have you checked the prices? Any comments?

The rotary tillers we quoted are specially designed for the Thailand market. Quality components are used to ensure its stable performance. I'm sure it will be well-received in your market.[2]

If you have any requirements or concerns, please let me know.

Yours,
Rong Jiaping

Comments

1. 在写跟进邮件时,可以不新建邮件,而是选择"回复"我方上一封回复此客户询盘的邮件。这样第一次发给客户的邮件内容就在本邮件下方(也就是保留了之前的邮件往来记录),可以提示买家第一次邮件内容。也可以修改上次的邮件主题,从不同方面突出我方优势。

2. 强调我方的优势,可再次强调上一封邮件中所写的优势,也可写新的内容。

Sample 2　the second follow-up email

Subject: Re: Re: Reply to Inquiry/Quotation for Rotary Tillers Valid before April 20[1]

Dear Mr. Adirake Phupoom,

Good day.

This is Jiaping from Zeyi, Machinery. Have you checked our offer of February 20? It's valid before April 20. Please note we've quoted a very competitive price. As casting iron price is likely to go up recently, we suggest you hurry with your order.[2]

I have attached a catalogue of our latest hot sale products. Competitive prices will be quoted if you have new inquiries.

Let me know if you have any questions.

Sincerely,
Rong Jiaping

Comments

1. 在邮件主题突出报盘有效期,为此作为跟进的理由。

2. 在正文中再次强调报价有效期,告诉客户现在生产的原材料比较便宜,如果现在安排生产,价格就可以比较低,之后可能会涨价。

Sample 3 the third follow-up email

Subject: Re: Re: Reply to Inquiry/Quotation for Rotary Tillers

Dear Mr. Adirake Phupoom,

How is everything?

How is your order for rotary tillers? If still pending, as the cultivation season is soon to come, please order soon so that we can arrange production and shipment as soon as possible.[1]

I'd like to call you for a discussion. Is 10:30 March 4 (your time) a good time? Please reply "Yes" if it is.[2]

Yours,
Rong Jiaping

Comments

1. 将交货期作为跟进的理由。在价格有效期内,以交货期为由,给客户一点压力,催促其尽快下单。

2. 提出打电话给他,直接给个时间问他意见(但不要选择客户早上刚上班或快下班的时间)。此处为客户着想,让他简单回答"Yes"即可。

Section 3 Core Phrases and Sentence Patterns

(1) I'm following up on the proposal/quotation/offer I sent you on July 27. I've attached a copy below.

(2) Have you had a chance to look over the quote I sent you on July 27?

(3) I want to follow up, and see if you've had a chance to review my previous email.

(4) Have you checked the proposal? Any comments?

(5) How about getting back together and establishing a plan for moving forward with the proposal I sent you?

(6) We're eager to hear your thoughts, and get started on this project! Please let me know if you have any questions regarding the specifics of the proposal.

(7) I'd love to organize a quick call to talk it over in more detail. Would Tuesday 3 p.m. work for you?

(8) It would be great to have a conversation on the phone and that we can have a catch-up about your current needs. How does 3 p.m. Tuesday sound?

外贸业务员如何报价

1. 报价策略

（1）Leave some room for negotiation. 第一次报价给自己留有适当空间。

（2）Quote a reasonable price. 价格合理，太高或太低的报价都可能被客户直接忽略。

（3）Provide options. 根据客户提供的资料，设计出几套方案，建议客户用什么材料，做多大尺寸等，由客户做选择。这样我方就掌握了主动权，如同让客户做选择题，这不仅显示我方的专业度和强烈的服务意识，也避免与竞争对手同质竞争。

（4）给客户二次或多次报价时要不断更新报价单。

2. 关于报价单（quotation sheet）

（1）若产品只有一两款，可在正文中直接报价。

（2）若需报价的产品较多，除了在邮件正文写上重要信息，还可附上 PDF 报价单。一般不建议采用附件的方式报价，原因是附件有时会比较大，如果客户的网络条件不是很好，有可能会收不到；有些邮件服务器会自动屏蔽带有附件的邮件；很多客户对附件比较敏感，不会轻易打开带有附件的邮件。为了让客户一目了然，建议把报价直接放在邮件正文显眼的位置。

（3）若附报价单附件，可用 Excel 或者 Word 把字体、图片大小等都排版清楚美观后，转成 PDF 文件再放进邮件。

3. 报盘后的跟进

报盘后要跟进。跟进邮件的发送时间宜选择周二至周五。周一不适合跟进，因为周一上班后，客户的邮箱里往往会塞满需处理的工作邮件，难以有耐心仔细阅读此类业务开发邮件，效果会大打折扣。

客户收到了邮件之后没有任何回应，一般有以下几种原因。

（1）回复时间太迟，客户已收到其他供应商的邮件。由于存在时差，若在我方上班时间回复邮件，邮件交流有滞后性。

（2）我方报价在众多报价之中缺乏竞争力或者不是客户所需。竞争力体现在专业性、技术标准、价格、品质等方面。因此第一次报价时就应报出最有竞争力的方案，报价的技术规格也需要与客户的需求相匹配。此外，如果是技术参数、价格、产品质量这类我方可以解决的问题，要根据客户要求做出细致的方案。

（3）不可抗力因素导致采购取消或推迟。如市场环境突然发生变化，汇率大幅度下跌导致采购取消或推迟，甚至是采购人突然生病等意外情况。这类因素无法控制，唯一能做的是保持沟通，等待情况好转。

（4）有时，客户已经有成熟供应商，发询盘只是了解市场行情，以便与现有供应商还价。这时，随时保持有效沟通，则有希望成为主要备选供应商。

遇到对产品暂时不感兴趣或者没有采购需求的客户，可保持邮件沟通，给他发送产品的正面信息,如产品的出货和包装图片、最新的测试报告和获得的证书、其他客户的正面产品反馈等,激发其购买欲望。

Communication Laboratory

I. Fill in each of the following blanks with a proper word/words given in the box.

| series | superior | state-of-the-art | advantage | collection |
| fabric | customized | suit | demand | approach |

1. This _____ of product has a novel structure and stable performance.
2. A few years ago it was virtually impossible to find _____ quality coffee in local shops.
3. We are using _____(最新的)graphics in the film's special effects.
4. The jacket is comfortable because the _____(织物)breathes.
5. Besides those items above, we also produce _____(定制的)products requested by clients.
6. We may choose a soft, medium or firm mattress(床垫)to _____ their individual needs.
7. We have been _____ by a number of companies that are interested in our product.
8. BOSIDENG will be holding fashion shows to present their autumn _____.
9. Another _____ of our new series is reliability.
10. _____ for our machines has been on the increase for the past 6 months.

II. Please write up sentences based on the following situations.

1. 我方想给客户报儿童背包的价格。(quote … as follows)

_____

2. 我方想告诉客户,订购茶具超过1 000套,可享受5%优惠。(discount)

_____

3. 我方想告诉客户,我司有一巴西客户,多次续订该儿童背包。(repeated orders)

_____

4. 我方想告诉客户,本次报盘有效期是2021年1月3日(我方时间)。(remain valid till)

_____

5. 我方想以圣诞节临近为由,敦促对方尽早下单。(as … is approaching)

_____

6. 我们想以产品需求旺盛为由，敦促对方尽早下单。(heavy demand for)

III. Write an email in English based on the situation given.

Visit alibaba. com to search for a company selling laptop computer bags. Suppose you're the salesperson of this company, please make an offer (include an email subject) to the given inquiry.

An Inquiry

Good day Sir/Madam,

How are you doing today? Hope all is well. I am Carol from London.

I'm interested in your laptop computer bag (Model No. : YH-0132). I would like a competitive price. Please tell me the terms of payment. I want to purchase 3 000 pcs of the bags.

I await your fast response.

Regards,
Mrs. Carol Williams

Your reply to the above inquiry.

Subject

Content

Module 5 Counter-offers

模块 5 还盘

Learning Goals

- Know about how to analyze a counter-offer from the buyer.
- Know about the key points of replying to the buyer's counter-offers.
- Be able to reply to the buyer's counter-offer.

Lead-in

Situation: After sending an offer to a potential buyer, you now receive a counter-offer. How would you respond to the counter-offer?

Questions:

1. What are you supposed to do after receiving the counter-offer from the buyer?
2. What information shall be included in your reply to the buyer's counter-offer?

Writing a Counter-offer to the Seller

A counter-offer is a new offer made in response to an offer received. It's a partial rejection of the original offer.

After receiving an offer, if the buyer finds part or all of the conditions are unacceptable, he may show his disagreement and raise his terms instead, for further discussions about the terms of price, packing, shipment time, payment and so on. Thus the original firm offer becomes invalid and unbinding（无约束力）, and a new offer comes into being. This is a counter-offer. Then the original seller may make another counter-offer of his own. In complicated deals, this process can go on for several rounds till business is concluded or called off.

Section 1 Guidelines

Suppose you were now a buyer, would you accept a seller's first offer?

Of course not. In international trade, usually, there is some room for negotiation in the first offer. A buyer and a seller never accept the first offer made by the other side.

In writing a counter-offer letter, the buyer should state the counter-proposal explicitly (明确地). Since a counter-offer is a new offer, it should be written with good care.

Structure of a counter-offer according to the following part.

Opening: thanks for the offer.

Body:
- Rejection and reasons.
- The counter-proposal.

Closing: the expectation of acceptance.

Section 2 Samples

Sample 1   a counter-offer on price

Dear Mr. Rong,

Thank you for your offer of May 5 quoting for rotary tillers.[1]

We like your rotary tillers, but your prices appear to be on the high side compared with those of other makers.[2] We also have offers from several other manufacturers, all of which have quoted prices 10% to 15% below yours.

Could you consider reducing the price by, say 10%? We have a thorough knowledge of our market and excellent sales channels in Thailand. If the price is reasonable, we believe there will be repeated orders in the next cultivating season.[3] You may find it worthwhile to make a concession.

Looking forward to[4] your favorable reply.

Regards,
(Mr.)Adirake Phupoom

Comments

1. 引述对方的报盘并表达感谢。

2. 说明无法接受对方报盘的原因。

3. 提出自己的方案。在这封信中，买方以自己有销售渠道优势，未来能续订货为由，希望卖方在价格上让步。

4. 表达希望对方接受该还盘。

Core Vocabulary

on the high side	偏高
thorough	adj. 深入的，透彻的
channel	n. 渠道
concession	n. 让步
worthwhile	adj. 值得的

Sample 2　a counter-offer on price

Dear Morgan,

Thank you for your proposal of October 20. We appreciate your efforts in submitting such a comprehensive proposal for us.

We reviewed the proposal in detail, and overall we are happy with it.[1] However, our Vice President has given us a specific budget for this deal. We also got another three quotes from other suppliers. If we cannot get your price within our budget, we would have to shift to other suppliers.[2]

I would love to have you as our supplier with a better price. Your price should be 9% lower at a final price of USD500/pc.

I am sure that your flexibility should result in more future cooperation between us.[3]

Looking forward to hearing from you by November 28.[4]

Best Regards,
James

Comments

1. 感谢对方的报价，并肯定对方提出的方案。
2. 提出自己的难处，作为希望对方降价的理由。
3. 以未来更多合作为由，希望对方这次能在价格上灵活处理。
4. 给出回复期限。

Core Vocabulary

proposal	*n.* 提议；提案
specific	*adv.* 明确的；具体的
comprehensive	*adj.* 综合的
budget	*n.* 预算
review	*v. /n.* 审查；检查
flexibility	*n.* 灵活性

Sample 3   a counter-offer on shipment

Dear Miss Lin,

Overall, your offer dated November 2 is acceptable to us. Since we would proceed to launch a sales campaign, please kindly advance the time of shipment before March 10, 2021.[1]

If this modification is possible without affecting other terms and conditions in your offer, we are planning to place an order with you.[2]

Looking forward to hearing from you soon.

Sincerely yours,
Johnson Smiths

Comments

1. 总体同意对方报价，但以很快要进行营销活动为由，希望交货期提前。
2. 提出自己的还盘意见，即交货期提前，但其他条款保持不变。

Core Vocabulary

overall	*adv.* 大致上，总体上
proceed to do sth.	接着做
campaign	*n.* （为社会、商业或政治目的而进行的一系列有计划的）活动
modification	*n.* 修改

Section 3   Core Phrases and Sentence Patterns

1. Express thanks for the offer

- Thank you for your email of March 10 quoting for LED lights.
- Thank you for your offer of September 20 for men's leather bags.

2. Express rejection and state reasons

- Regrettably, we are unable to accept your offer as your prices are too high.
- Unfortunately, your price appears to be on the high side for goods of this quality.
- We like the quality and design of your products, but they do not justify such a price difference.
- If we cannot get your price within our budget, we would have to shift to other suppliers.
- Your prices are higher than those of other makers.
- Your price is higher than we expected.
- We are a little worried about the prices you're asking for.
- It is much higher than that of other suppliers.
- Your quotation is unworkable/out of line with the prevailing market(现行市场).

3. State counter-proposal

- Could you consider reducing the price by, say 10%?
- We might do business with you if you could give us a 20% discount.
- We will place an order with you if you could lower the price by 10%.

4. Express expectation of acceptance

- We shall appreciate your favorable reply.
- Awaiting your favorable reply.
- I hope to get your acceptance of this offer.
- Looking forward to hearing from you by October 30.

Task 2

Writing a Re-counteroffer to the Buyer

Now, if we were the seller, what shall we do after receiving a counter-offer from the buyer?

A letter may be written to reply to the buyer's counter-offer. This is part of the negotiation process. The tone of the reply letter needs to be polite and informative. We could point out how much a specific product costs, what the quotation encompasses(包含), or what value can the product bring to the customer. This reply letter can be used to give the customer an idea of why we cannot reduce the price of a product or a service to the requested level.

Section 1 Guidelines

1. Preparations before the task

After receiving a counter-offer from the buyer, the seller may take the following steps.

(1) *Analyze the counter-offer letter*

Although most counter-offer(especially in the first round of negotiation)are on price, it's not always the case. The buyer may show his disagreement and raise his terms about the terms of price, packing, shipment time, payment and so on. We need to read the counter-offer letter to find out the buyer's disagreement and his terms.

Before proceeding to write a re-counter offer to state our proposal, make sure we know something about the buyer, so that we may understand and estimate the buyer's needs and objectives and prepare feasible responses to his objections. In the meantime, we also figure out which is more important for us: to sell our export product to the buyer to make more profit, or to build a long-term business relationship? Having answered the questions, we may then define the limit of the potential agreement, i. e., decide the maximum(最多)and minimum(最少)we can give up as a compromise(妥协)to reach an agreement.

(2) *Make a re-counteroffer*

In the re-counteroffer letter, we may clarify why we can't accept the buyer's counter-offer. The reasons can be our price is in line with the market, or there has been a rise in raw material prices, labor cost, production cost, transportation cost, sales cost, etc.

We can clarify the basis of our quotation, what the quotation encompasses, such as specification(规格), model, contents of ingredients(成分含量), services provided.

We can highlight superior quality or services and provide more options for the buyer in terms of different grades of quality, materials, packaging, terms of payment, order quantity, etc.

We should specify a term or condition in exchange for a concession. In negotiations, make sure we get something for giving something.

2. Structure of a reply to buyer's counter-offer

Opening: thanks for the counter-offer.

Body:

- Rejection and reasons.
- A new proposal.

Closing: the expectation of acceptance.

Section 2 Samples

Sample 1

To: adirake_phupoom@yahoo.com
From: rong_jiaping@zeyimachinery.com
Subject: Re: Re: Your Counter-offer on Rotary Tillers of Zeyi[1]

Dear Mr. Phupoom,

Thank you for your email of July 10. We regret to learn that since other suppliers are offering at lower prices, you are unable to accept our offer.[2]

Over the last 10 years, Zeyi has managed to keep its prices competitive despite the ever-rising costs. We believe that even in today's world, we remain quite competitive for what we offer to our customers.

We wonder whether other suppliers are offering quality as good as ours. We ask you to note that we use materials of premium quality and offer value-added services such as[3]
- a short lead time
- one-year warranty
- free technical support

We regret to say that we are unable to accept your counter-offer. The best we can offer is a 5% discount.[4]

We await your early reply.[5]

Sincerely yours,
Rong Jiaping

Comments

1. 若对方之前的还盘邮件没有写上比较清晰明了的邮件主题，回复时可对其进行修改，让对方一目了然。
2. 感谢对方的还盘，用"regret to learn"句型表达遗憾之情，并简述其还盘信的主要内容。
3. 说明我方报价的基础，即使用了质量好的材料，有附加服务。
4. 提出我方的方案。
5. 希望对方尽早回复。

Core Vocabulary

ever-rising	不断上升的
premium	*adj.* 优质的，高端的

Sample 2

To: Doraraj@Dedocy.com
From: linhua111@163.com
Subject: Re: Re: Re: Counter-offer on Football Jerseys of Tontos

Dear Doraraj,

Thank you for your email of May 20, and we are sorry to learn you find our prices too high.[1]

Unfortunately, we are unable to comply with your request for a 20% discount. Our prices are carefully calculated. We have received a lot of orders from other buyers, which shows that our prices are reasonable. [2]

In view of our friendly cooperation, we're prepared to give you a 5% discount on Bob's Collection. Please note this is the best we can do. [3]

We'd like to recommend our 112K Collection. This collection can be an excellent substitute for Bob's Collection and sells at the price much closer to what you wish to pay. We are prepared to grant you a 10% discount on it to help you introduce it to the market. Attached is its price list. If you are interested, please let us know. [4]

We are looking forward to receiving your order ASAP. [5]

Sincerely yours,
Lin Hua

Comments

1. 感谢对方的还盘，用"sorry to learn"句型表达遗憾之情，并简述其还盘信的主要内容。
2. 明确说明我方不能接受对方的要求，用其他买家的例子说明我方报价合理。
3. 提出我方的方案，最多降价5%。
4. 推荐价格较低但与之前所报产品类似的其他产品供对方选择。
5. 希望尽早收到对方的订单。

Core Vocabulary

comply with	遵从
calculate	v. 计算
in view of	由于，鉴于
substitute	n/v. 替代

Sample 3

Subject: Re: Re: Re: Counter-offer on TDox K Series Bulk Order

Dear Mr. Phillips:

Thank you for your counter-offer of May 23 on the price reduction of your TDox-K Series bulk order. We called a meeting to discuss your request and deliberated on every way in which we could reduce this cost.

Please refer to the following facts that explain why this is not possible.

- TDox K Series is an innovative technology that our competitors are selling at a price 15% higher than we are in bulk orders.
- Our profit stands very low at the price we have offered to you. [1]

Considering these two, I'm afraid we cannot reduce the price of your bulk order by 15% as you requested. However, to make things easier for you, we are willing to offer a 5% discount and advance the delivery of your order by 15 days, that is, delivery can be made before August 20, 2020. [2]

Please let me know if this is a viable solution so that we can process your order further. [3]

Thank you very much.

Sincerely,
Henry Egro

Comments

1. 说明我方不能接受对方的要求的原因。
2. 说明我方的方案，即最多降价5%，并提前15天交货。
3. 希望对方回复该方案是否可行。

Core Vocabulary

bulk order	大批订货
innovative	*adj.* 革新的；创新的
deliberate	*v.* 仔细考虑；深思熟虑
viable	*adj.* 切实可行的

Sample 4

Subject: Re: Re: Re: 3% Lower in Price for USB Rechargeable LED Flashlights [1]

Dear Henry,

Thank you for your email replying to our offer on our USB rechargeable LED flashlights.

We have been providing our LED flashlights using quality materials at competitive prices to our valued customers since 2007. We assure you of the least possible pricing for our products.[2]

If the price we previously quoted is not suitable for you, would you accept a little change on it? The original length of the flashlight is 105mm, and now we make it shorter, 91mm instead. All the luminosity and the body look the same, and there's no need to worry about quality. Because of the material saved, the price will be EUR 2.13/pc, 3% lower.[3]

I think it's workable for both of us. Any comments?[4]

Best regards,
Janet Yang

Comments

1. 在邮件主题写出正文大意。
2. 强调我方定价合理。
3. 提出能使价格降低的建议。
4. 希望对方回复该方案是否可行。

Core Vocabulary

rechargeable	*adj.* 可再充电的
valuable	*adj.* 有价值的，宝贵的

Extended Vocabulary

flashlight	*n.* 手电筒
luminosity	*n.* 光度；亮度

Section 3　Core Phrases and Sentence Patterns

1. Express thanks for the counter-offer

（1）Thank you for your email of …（日期）. We are sorry/regret to learn that …（简述对方信件的主要意思）.

- Thank you for your email of April 9. We are sorry to learn you find our prices too high.
- Thank you for your email of July 10. We regret to learn that since other suppliers are offering at lower prices, you are unable to accept our offer.

（2）Thank you for your prompt reply to our offer. We regret to learn that …（简述对方信件的主要意思）.

（3）Thanks for getting back to us. We are sorry to learn that …（简述对方信件的主要

Module 5 Counter-offers
模块 5 还盘

意思).

2. Say that we cannot accept the counter-offer

- Regrettably, we are unable to supply the goods at the price indicated in your email.
- Unfortunately, we are unable to comply with your request.
- We're afraid we cannot accept your counter-offer.

3. State reasons why we cannot accept buyer's counter-offer

(1) Say that the price is reasonable.

- Our price is entirely in line with the prevailing market.
- The price is going up because of the rise in production cost.
- The world market for this item shows an upward trend. There may be a further rise in price soon.
- As the labor cost is increasing now, it would be hardly profitable for us if we offer a 10% discount.
- Considering(In view of)the high quality, our price is very reasonable.

(2) clarify the basis of our quotation, highlight the quality of our product or make a comparison with competitors.

- Please note that the material we use is of the top grade.
- We are using raw materials of premium quality.
- Please compare the material we used with those used by other suppliers. We believe you can see the difference.
- It's(lighter, more stylish, more durable…)than some products of its kind.

(3) Provide more options for the buyer.

- We provide two grades for you to choose from:
  A grade, USD ×××, with a special discount of ×××
  B grade, USD ×××, similar to A grade, with a price much more competitive.
- We'd like to recommend…(另一个产品). It can be an excellent substitute for…(之前报价产品).

(4) Specify a term or condition in exchange for a compromise.

- If you increase your order to 3 000 sets, we would consider giving you a 10% discount.
- If you can guarantee payment of 50% down-payment within 5 days of order, we can give you an additional 5% discount.
- We accept your proposal, on the condition that you order 20 000 units.

(5) Mention an example of other clients.

- We have received a lot of orders from other buyers, which shows that our prices are reasonable.
- Since we have done a lot of business with buyers at this price, we cannot reduce our price any further.

(6) Exert pressure.

- Frankly speaking, we can't make any profit with the price you offer.
- If you insist on a 20% reduction in price, we're afraid we don't see a business chance.
- The best we can do is to reduce our previous quotation by 2%.
- Please note this is the best we can do and we hope you will accept it.

4. Express expectation

- We will appreciate your understanding in this matter.
- We would appreciate receiving your reply as soon as possible.
- We look forward to entering into business with you.
- If you would like further information, please call me at 555-5555.
- I would like to call you to discuss this matter further. Is 10:30 Wednesday morning (your time) a good time for you?

Task 3

Following up after Replying to the Buyer's Counter-offer

After negotiation, we must always carry out all of the follow-up actions. If not, all our negotiating efforts could go to waste.

Section 1 Guidelines

Receiving answers to emails makes salespeople feel successful. Sometimes, after sending a reply to counter-offers, there's no response. We may test out a few of these tactics(策略) in our follow-up outreach and see if they make a difference in our response rates.

1. Include a closing in our email

When we send an initial follow-up email to fish for a response, we may throw in an "I'd love to hear back from you" or "I'd like to learn more about what you think". In the meantime, make sure we give our prospect an opening to respond. Include firm questions like

- Are you free for a conversation this Friday, August 28?
- Can you return feedback on the proposal by next Tuesday, September 1?

2. Always send a fresh email

Never cut and paste or forward the original email. This leaves our emails vulnerable to being filtered by spam or blocked entirely. Try new subject lines, opening greetings, and call to action.

Section 2 Samples

Sample 1 follow-up after sending proforma invoice

Subject: Please Sign and Confirm PI of Rotary Tiller from Zeyi [1]

Hi Mr. Adirake Phupoom,

Nice day!

I sent you a PI on March 20, and now I'm sending it to you again. Would you please sign and confirm asap? We need plenty of time to arrange mass production. [2]

It's a long time since I got your last reply. How is everything going? Please keep me informed of any further development. [3]

Thanks and best regards,
Jiaping

Comments

1. 在邮件主题栏写明需要对方做什么，一目了然。此次是之前与客户谈好价格后，卖方做好 PI(proforma invoice) 让客户确认。PI 发过去后，没有回音，此时卖方进行跟进。
2. 给出跟进的理由，大批量生产需要及早安排。
3. 希望对方告知进展。

Core Vocabulary

PI(proforma invoice)	形式发票
mass production	大批量生产
keep sb. informed of sth.	告知某人某事

Sample 2 follow-up to schedule a call

Subject: Is 10:30 Sept. 25 Thursday A Good Time to Call? [1]

Hello Doraraj,

Hope your week is going well.

Regarding your concerns about the prices of sports jerseys, I think Tontos can help you improve your competitive edge in your market.

I'd love to tell you a few of my ideas over a 15-minute call. Is 10:30 September 25 Thursday a good time?[2]

Thanks,
Jeff

Comments

1. 在邮件主题写出正文大意。

2. 与对方商定打电话时间时，详细列出时间，对方只需回复"Yes"或另外指定时间即可，减少对方的麻烦，提升回复率。若邮件系统有插入日历的功能，可将日历插入正文，让对方选择一个时间。

Core Vocabulary

competitive edge   竞争优势

Sample 3 follow-up after a call

Subject: More about How We Can Help[1]

Hi Doraraj,

It was nice that we discussed your concerns on our last call. It's helpful for me to learn more about your sales target for this year.[2] I understand the challenges you're encountering and how they make it harder to earn a better market share.

As mentioned, I've attached more information about how we can help you be more competitive in the market.[3]

Just let me know if you have any questions and I'd be happy to chat again. I look forward to talking again on 15:30 September 30 next Tuesday[4].

Best regards,
Jeff

Comments

1. 这是与潜在客户打完电话之后的跟进邮件。邮件主题"More about How We Can Help"有利于吸引对方的注意。

2. 总结之前电话对话的内容和成果。

3. 附上可能对对方有帮助的信息。

4. 期待下次再一次谈话，与对方确认下次谈话时间。

Core Vocabulary

concern	n. 担心, 忧虑
encounter	v. 遭遇；遇到（尤指令人不快或困难的事）
market share	市场份额

Sample 4 follow-up to ask about the sample

Subject: Pls Confirm the Sample from Kontos[1]

Dear Doraraj,

Do you have a final decision on our samples? We need your comments to go ahead.[2]

Thank you!

Kind regards,
Jeff
Kontos Ltd.

Comments

1. 在邮件主题中敦促对方行动。
2. 言简意赅地说明需要对方做什么，原因是什么。

Core Vocabulary

go ahead	进行；开展（某项工作）

Section 3 Core Phrases and Sentence Patterns

1. Greet the recipient

- Nice day!
- How is everything going?
- Hope your week is going well.

2. State the purpose of the email

(1) I'm writing to…

- I'm writing to ask about our samples.
- I'm writing to ask for your comments on our offer.

(2) Regarding…, I think we can…

- Regarding your concerns about the price, I think we can help you improve your competitive edge in your market.

(3) I'd love to…/I'd be happy to…

- I'd love to tell you a few of my ideas over a 15-minute call.
- We'd love to have your comments.

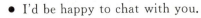

- I'd be happy to chat with you.

3. Close the email

- Are you free to chat this Friday, August 28?
- Could you return feedback on our proposal by next Tuesday, September 1?
- Please keep me informed of any further development.
- Is 10:30 Sep. 25 Thursday a good time for me to call you?

如何回应客户的降价要求？

价格通常是商务谈判中最敏感的问题。在报价及谈判时，应先明确其他方面的条件与条款，最后在此基础上定价。报价后，买方可能敦促卖方在如下方面做出让步：价格降低；价格不变，但产品或服务的质量更高；重复订单可享受折扣；价格相同的基础上改进包装；交货期限缩短；独家经销权；长期代理；提高佣金率；将付款条件改成对买方更有利等。

出口商首先应设法确定买方最关注的问题，从而针对对方的还盘意见提出可行的对策。

当客户想表达"I'm going to need a better price"或"The price is too high"时，他们经常使用以下措辞。

1. Wow, that's a lot. Can we do it for less?

不管我们给出什么价格，有些客户的第一反应始终是要求价格更低。此时，我们应当明确我方的报价依据。

- The cost of this solution encompasses best-in-class customer service and experienced support 24/7. （我们所报方案的价格包括一流的客户服务以及一天24小时、周末无休、经验丰富的售后支持。）
- Our offer may not be the cheapest one available, but our solution is the best—and that's a claim backed up by our team winning the "Best Customer Service" award three years in a row. （我们的方案也许不是最便宜的，但是绝对是最好的——我方团队连续三年获得"最佳客户服务"奖，这就是证明。）

2. It costs too much. Money is going to be a problem.

买方可能会担心：我有必要增加××%的支出吗？这些所谓质量更好的产品/服务，真的值得我多付钱吗？他们能给我带来多大的收益？此时，我们可以回答："I understand your concern. I have many clients who had similar budget constraints but saw huge gains in revenue after buying from us.（我了解您的担忧。我有许多客户和您一样，也有预算方面的限制，但是从我们这里购买后获得了巨大的收益。）"

通过分享背景相似的客户的故事，有助于减少客户的疑虑。

3. I received other proposals and your price is the highest.

如果我们熟悉市场行情，那么应该明白客户这种说法是否站得住脚。无论如何，潜在客户很可能会以此作为讨价还价的筹码。

在这种情况下，我们应该突出我方产品或服务的价值，而不是盲目降价。应对这类说辞，我们可以提出改变报价里的一些条件条款，如数量、服务水平、保修条款等，从而达到对方所说的降价要求。

Communication Laboratory

I. Fill in each of the following blanks with a proper word/words given in the box. For some of the blanks, you may have more than one choice.

proceed	worthwhile	regrettably	justify	substitute
budget	comment	comply	workable	campaign

1. Building a negotiation team requires careful consideration and planning, but the benefits may be well _____.

2. We need to _____ our offer by listing out the reasons why we quote at this price.

3. In negotiations, we _____ with reasonable requests from the other side.

4. We may write to ask for _____ on the new proposals.

5. Negotiation is a need-to-have skill in business. _____, far too many of us lack effective negotiation skills.

6. We may point out the huge gain if buying from us to counter the "_____ constraints" excuse from our customers.

7. A sales _____ is a great way to increase demand for your product in a short amount of time.

8. After analyzing the concerns of the prospect, we may _____ to negotiate the deal based on the estimates(预估;判断).

9. Please let me know whether the suggestion is _____.

10. We may recommend a _____ design to reduce costs.

II. Read the sentences and fill in the blanks with proper prepositions.

1. We regret to learn that since other suppliers are offering _____ lower prices, you are unable to accept our offer.

2. _____ the last 6 years, we have managed to keep our prices competitive despite the ever-rising costs.

3. We wonder whether other suppliers are offering a quality _____ good _____ ours. We ask you to note that we use materials _____ premium quality and offer value-added services.

4. We regret to say that we're unable to comply _____ your requests.

5. In view _____ our longstanding business relationship, we accept your counter-offer.

6. Reduced-calorie cheese is a great substitute _____ cream cheese.

7. Our profit stands very low _____ the price we have offered _____ you.

8. I am afraid we cannot reduce the price _____ your bulk order _____ 15% as you requested.

9. We assure you _____ the least possible pricing for our products.

10. Please keep me informed _____ any further development.

III. Please write up sentences based on the following situations.

1. 对方 8 月 15 日发来电子邮件,认为我方报价过高,不能接受,回信的第一句可以怎么写?(Thank you for…We regret/are sorry to learn that…)

2. 你希望对方注意,我方不仅材料质量优越,还提供 3 年的免费保修(warranty)。

3. 你希望对方注意,我方产品是同类产品中质量最好的(the best of its kind)。

4. 我方拟同意降价 10%,但想让对方把订货量增加到 3 000 件。

5. 我方拟同意再降价 3%,条件是对方在下单后 10 个工作日内支付 40% 首付款(down payment),可以跟对方怎么说?

6. 我方拟推荐 TEX 系列给对方,想跟对方说 TEX 系列可以很好地代替 DOK 系列。(recommend…substitute for…)

7. 在 email 的最后,我方想让对方告知方案是否可行。(proposal, workable/viable)

8. 我方想跟对方确认可否下周四 15:30 打电话给他。(is…a good time?)

IV. Write an email in English based on the situation given.

1. Suppose your sales team receives a counter-offer from a buyer asking you to reduce the price by 20%. One of your colleagues drafted a reply as below. How is the reply? How would you revise it?

A reply to the buyer's counter-offer

Module 5　Counter-offers
模块 5　还盘

> Dear ×××,
>
> Thanks for your email of ×××.
>
> I make the price list again. A big discount on them. But the quality of them is lower than the original goods.
>
> Best regards,
> ×××

Your comments on the above reply.

How would you revise the above email? Please write your revised version here.

Subject

Content

2. You receive a counter-offer from a buyer as below. Please draft a reply to it.
The Buyer's Counter-offer

Dear Derrick:

Thanks for your offer on LED lights.

We regret to say your price is too high! You quoted me EUR2.35, but my competitor bought a very similar one from a middle man in Germany at just EUR2.15.

There's no way we can do business unless you cut your price down to that level, at EUR2.15.

Looking forward to your reply.

Frank

Your reply to the above email.

Module 6 Dealing with Orders

模块6 订单处理

Learning Goals

- Be familiar with typical expressions and sentence patterns used in order-related correspondence.
- Be able to write English emails/messages related to processing orders and sending samples.

Lead-in

Situation: You're a salesperson. Now you receive an order from a South-American company.

Questions:

1. What are you supposed to do after receiving an order?
2. What information shall be included when confirming or declining an order?
3. What preparations would you make before mass production?

Task 1　Responding to Orders

An order is a request from the buyer to the seller to supply some particular goods. Before responding to an order, the seller should scrutinize(仔细检查)all the information in the order, such as the description of goods, specifications, quantity, unit price, packing, time of shipment, payment terms, etc., to ensure fulfillment of the order afterwards.

Section 1 Guidelines

1. Compass

There are some guidelines to follow after receiving an order.

(1) Scrutinize all items in the order before confirming

Upon receipt of the order from the buyer, the seller should examine all items in the order carefully. In case there's anything inconsistent(不一致的) with the previous discussion or the seller can't execute, the seller should raise it for clarification/discussion with the buyer.

(2) A sales confirmation/contract can protect the seller better

When confirming the buyer's order, in most cases, the seller, together with the buyer, should sign a contract or sales confirmation, prepared by the seller. The Contract or Sales Confirmation may protect the seller better than an order only, because normally it contains clauses such as inspection clause, claim clause, arbitration and force majeure(不可抗力) clause and the like, which can protect the seller better in case of any dispute arising from the deal.

2. Writing structure

(1) Accepting an order

If we accept buyer's order, we need to send him/her an email to acknowledge the order. This acknowledgement email also gives us an opportunity to offer more information about our company, and thus can be an effective sales tool and a way of furthering customer relations.

An order acknowledgment email should include the following contents.

① Thank the customer for the order.

② Review the contents of the order.

③ Give additional details.

(2) Declining an order

Declining a customer's order isn't pleasant, but it's an issue most businesses face sooner or later. Maybe we don't have the supplies or the stock, maybe the size of the order is too small that it gives little profit, maybe we simply can't work within such a short time frame, or maybe we're spending our resources elsewhere. Whatever the case, it's important to be respectful and professional when communicating the bad news to the client. We should write a short letter to reveal why we are not accepting the order to maintain our relationship with the client.

An email to decline an order may include the following contents.

① Extend the gratefulness for the order.

② Provide a reason why we are not able to deliver the request. Make the explanation short yet understandable.

③ End the letter positively.

(3) Declining an order but providing a substitute item

In case we cannot supply a product ordered, when refusing a client's request, we can use the chance to introduce a substitute to the client.

An email to decline an order but provide a substitute item may be written like this.

① Express gratitude to the client for placing the order.

② If possible, provide an explanation on why we cannot attend the request or order. Write it using the passive voice, if needed, so there is no one to be blamed. Shortly point out that the item he ordered is not available.

③ Introduce the substitute item pleasantly, show the similarity of features it has to the original item ordered such as lower prices, the speed of delivery, etc.

④ Provide the reader a more simple way on how to order the substitute item.

⑤ End the letter positively.

Section 2 Samples

Sample 1 place an order

Subject: Order for USB Rechargeable LED Flashlights

Dear Mr. Zhang,

Thank you for your email replying to our counter-offer on USB rechargeable LED flashlights.

EUR 2.13/pc is workable for us. Attached is our Purchase Order No. HFS1263.

We will open an irrevocable sight L/C in your favor through our banker for the total value of $128 000 as stated in this order. Kindly advise us of the shipping date at least 10 days in advance after receipt of our L/C.

We look forward to your confirmation of our order.

Bast regards,
Bill Bush

Core Vocabulary

in one's favor	以某方为受益人
irrevocable sight L/C	不可撤销即期信用证

Sample 2 accept an order (reply to Sample 1)

Subject: Order HSF1263

Dear Mr. Bush,

Thank you for your order No. HSF1263. We are pleased to confirm that we sell you

1 000 pieces of USB rechargeable LED flashlights CIF New York with shipment in June 2020.

Attached is our Sales Contract No. GJ6283 in PDF. Kindly countersign and return one copy to us for our file.

Upon receipt of your relevant L/C, we will arrange shipment and advise you of the shipping date ASAP.

Yours faithfully,
Henry Zhang

Comments

出口商在收到进口商的订单后,一般会自己制作销售合同,给对方签署后存档,以方便把自己常用的包装、索赔、仲裁等条款写入销售合同中,更好地保护自身利益。

Core Vocabulary

countersign	v. 会签(文件)
relevant	adj. 相关的
for one's file	供某一方存档

Sample 3 place an order

Subject: New Order for Mountain Bikes

Dear Ms. Wang,

We'd like to order from you 3 000 sets of mountain bikes with details as below.

Quantity	Model No.	Unit Price (FOB Guangzhou)	Shipment Date
1 000 sets	76812	US $ 126/Set	Before October 1, 2020
1 000 sets	76826	US $ 136/Set	Before October 1, 2020
1 000 sets	76832	US $ 145/Set	Before October 1, 2020

Payment is by 100% T/T 15 days before shipment.

We understand such products are in stock, thus your prompt shipment is expected. Our order sheet is attached to this email for your confirmation. If this order proves satisfactory, substantial orders will follow.

Your prompt response is awaited.

Yours truly,
Jack White

Core Vocabulary

in stock	有存货
order sheet	订单
for one's confirmation	供某方确认
substantial	*adj.* 大量的

Sample 4 accept an order（reply to Sample 3）

Subject: New Order for Mountain Bikes

Dear Mr. White,

Thank you for your order of mountain bikes. We are pleased to accept your order except for the model 76832, which is very popular in the market and out of stock owing to heavy demand at present. We deeply regret that we can not meet your needs for this item at present. Once it is available, we will advise you without any delay.

Attached is the PI for your confirmation. We would appreciate your favorable response.

Best Regards,
Mei Wang

Core Vocabulary

except for	除了……以外
out of stock	脱销
owing to	由于，因为
heavy demand	大量需求

Sample 5 decline an order

Subject: Refusal of Order No. KV31/04

Dear Sirs,

We thank you for your order No. KV31/04 dated March 1, 2020, for 1 000 packets of Apple Juice.

To our regret, the size of your order is far below our required minimum of 3 000 packets. Our apple juice is of superior quality, and we have confidence that it will sell fast in your market. If you increase your order to 3 000 packets, we will be delighted to process it immediately and ship it as required.

Looking forward to your favorable reply.

Yours faithfully,
Donald Rafique(Mr.)

Core Vocabulary

packet   n. (商品的)小包装纸袋，小硬纸板盒

Sample 6   decline an order but provide a substitute item

Subject: Order for Super Pulsing Blenders

Dear Mr. Paul Carson,

Thank you for your order for Super Pulsing Blenders. The Super Pulsing Blender has been one of our top sellers for the past five years—customers love the stability of the machine, its attractive design, and multi-functions.

Now after five years, the Super Pulsing Blender II has been released—with numerous blending improvements including a juicing attachment, effectively giving you two machines in one! The Super Pulsing Blender II has been so well received that the Super Pulsing Blender, which you ordered, has been discontinued and is no longer available. We apologize for this inconvenience but can assure you that all customers who have spent the additional $5.00 and purchased the Super Pulsing Blender II have been more than happy with their decision. It also comes with our standard satisfaction guarantee and a two-year warranty on service and parts.

We will process your order immediately after you confirm to purchase the Super Pulsing Blender II.

Doing business with you is important to us, and we hope to hear from you soon.

Sincerely,
Xu Jialin(Miss)

Module 6　Dealing with Orders
模块 6　订单处理

Core Vocabulary

stability	n. 稳定性
attachment	n. （机器的）附件，附加装置
juice	n. 果汁，菜汁
	v. 榨出（水果或蔬菜的）汁液
discontinue	v. （使）终止，中断，中止

Extended Vocabulary

Super Pulsing Blender　　　超级脉冲搅拌机

Section 3　Core Phrases and Sentence Patterns

1. **Placing orders**
- We are pleased to place an order with you for 1 000 sets of Electric Toothbrush.
- Please supply the corresponding goods as per our order No. 326 attached.

2. **Accepting orders**
- We're pleased to accept your Order No. 8926.
- Thank you for your Order No. 236, and we're pleased to confirm that we will sell you the following items.
- Referring to the goods ordered under your Order No. 322, we have decided to accept your order at the same price as last quarter.

3. **Declining orders**
- We regret that we cannot accept your order owing to heavy commitments.
- We regret our inability to accept your order because of heavy bookings.
- Due to heavy demand, we are not in a position to accept orders requiring shipment in July.
- We regret to say that the smartwatch TEX1 you ordered has been discontinued and is no longer available. We'd like to recommend you the improved model TEX2.

Task 2　Preparing Pre-production Samples

The Pre-Production Sample (PPS) or Pre-Pro is a sample of the products that occur before manufacturing starts.

The pre-production sample helps buyers look over the design or any other manufacturing processes that need to be confirmed before large-scale production begins.

Pre-production samples allow both the manufacturer and the buyer to be entirely in agreement about the construction of the product. Once the PPS sample has been approved, the product can then move into manufacturing for the entire order.

Section 1 Guidelines

1. Prepare the pre-production samples as per requirements of contract or customers

In some lines of business, for example, fabric products, toys, leather products, etc., pre-production samples usually are required to send to the buyer before mass production. In that case, the seller or manufacturer should prepare and send such samples in compliance with the requirements of the contract or clients.

2. Revise the sample in accordance with the feedback of the customer

Normally, after receipt of pre-production samples, the buyer will examine them and communicate with the seller whether such samples are acceptable. Then the seller should discuss with the buyer for the comment and revise samples accordingly.

Section 2 Samples

Sample 1   give instruction about pre-production sample arrangement

Subject: PP Sample under S/C 20200616

Dear Mr. Zhang,

About the Sales Confirmation No. 20200616, we would like you to send us a pre-production sample of Backpacks for Women Art. No. S5261 before mass production. Kindly arrange to send the following specifications to our address below.

Colour: Elephant Skin Pattern Gray, Oil Wax Bright Brown, Living Coral

Our address: Maple Leaf Gifts Inc., No. 206 Glen Scarlett Road, Toronto, Canada M6N 1P5.

As the shipment date is pressing, your prompt response will be appreciated.

Best regards,
Bill

Comments

有些行业，例如服装、玩具、箱包等，签订合同后，在大规模生产之前，进口商会要求出口商先制作少量样品来看看质量是否符合要求，这些样品就是生产前样本，又称产前样。

Module 6　Dealing with Orders
模块 6　订单处理

Core Vocabulary

pre-production sample	生产前样本
backpack	n. 双肩背包，背包
mass production	大量生产
specification	n. 规格；说明书；详述
pressing	adj. 紧迫的，迫切的

Extended Vocabulary

Elephant Skin Pattern Gray	大象皮纹灰色
Oil Wax Bright Brown	油蜡亮棕色
Living Coral	珊瑚红

Sample 2　reply to Sample 1

Subject: Pre-production Sample under S/C 20200616

Dear Mr. Bush,

In response to your mail concerning the pre-production sample under S/C 20200616, please note that samples of Backpacks for Women Art. No. S5261 have been sent to you by DHL today, and the Tracking No. is DS2382628. Kindly advise us of your comment upon receipt.

We look forward to your early feedback.

Best regards,
Henry

Core Vocabulary

concerning	prep. 关于；就……而言
Tracking No.	查询号

Sample 3　follow up after sending a pre-production sample

Subject: Pre-production Sample under S/C 20200616

Dear Mr. Bush,

Good morning! Have you enjoyed the Thanksgiving Day?

Just to follow up on the samples we sent two weeks ago, have you received our samples? Do you find them satisfactory? We would appreciate your comment at your earliest convenience.

Should you have any questions, please let us know.

Best regards,
Henry

Core Vocabulary

satisfactory	*adj.* 满意的；符合要求的
comment	*n.* 评论；意见
convenience	*n.* 便利

Sample 4   reply to buyer's request to change the pre-pro sample

Subject: Pre-production Sample under S/C 20200616

Dear Mr. Bush,

Thanks for your feedback on the pre-production sample. A new sample exactly the same as that we provided at the Canton Fair will be prepared. It is expected to be completed in 3 days. We will send it to you within this week.

Hope to get your approval soon.

Best regards,
Henry

Section 3   Core Phrases and Sentence Patterns

Follow up after sending a sample

- Your sample has been sent out this morning by FedEx. The tracking No. is ×××. Track your shipment here: www.websitelink.com. Normally it can reach you within 6 working days.
- Just checked DHL, it has been received by Tom dated November 17, 2019.
- May I know if you have got it? If yes, is it OK?
- Just to follow up on the samples we sent two weeks ago, have you received our samples? Do you find them satisfactory?

- We would appreciate your comment at your earliest convenience.
- We look forward to your early feedback.

Tips

当必须拒绝客户订单时，要向客户表达遗憾之情，提出对方可以谅解的不能接受订单的原因，以维护双方的贸易关系。可使用 regret 一词，例如以下表述。

- We regret to advise that we cannot accept the order for the time being owing to heavy demands. We will inform you whenever a fresh supply becomes available.
- We regret to inform you that we cannot supply you with the goods within the time specified because our stock of Apple Juice has been exhausted and the replenishment of stock will take at least one month.

"regret"的意思是对某一行为或损失感到难过，表达的是一种"遗憾"和"惋惜"，并不一定代表自己这一方有过失。

若遭遇对方的投诉或索赔，且确实是我方过失，应承认自己的过失，请求对方谅解，此时用 sorry 或 apologize(程度由轻到重)。

- We are sorry for the trouble caused by the error.（对由此错误带给贵方的麻烦，我们非常抱歉。）
- We apologize for our mistakes and any inconvenience caused during the repairs.（对错误以及修理带来的不便道歉。）

Communication Laboratory

I. Fill in each of the following blanks with a proper word/words given in the box.

attached	countersign	mass
confirmation	owing to	tracking

1. We regret our inability to accept your order _____ heavy bookings.
2. We now email you our purchase order No. BUS1683 as per _____ file.
3. Please find our Sales Contract No. FL9762 in PDF. Kindly _____ and return one copy to us for our file.

4. We will prepare a pre-production sample of Backpacks for Women Art. No. GL6328 before _____ production.

5. Samples of smartwatch Art. No. WS2168 have been sent to you by FedEx today, and the _____ No. is FE25428.

6. A sample has been sent to you. Hope to get your _____ soon.

II. Translate the following sentences into English.

1. 我们很高兴地通知贵方，我们接受你们号码为 S3682 的订单。
   _____
   _____

2. 附件是我们 GL89236 号销售合同的 PDF 文档，请会签并寄回一份给我方存档。
   _____
   _____

3. 很抱歉，由于需求量大，我们不能接受 7 月装运的订单。
   _____
   _____

4. 请知悉，扫地机器人（robot cleaner）的样品今天已经通过 UPS 寄给你了，单号是 UP112628。
   _____
   _____

5. 对于半个月前寄给贵方的样品，贵方如能尽早给予评论，我们将不胜感激。
   _____
   _____

6. 我方已对样品进行以下修改并已重新发送样品，请贵方确认。
   _____
   _____

III. Write an email in English based on the situation given.

我方公司叫 DTDK Co., Ltd., 越南公司 GOMH Co., Ltd.（联系人：Mr. Ngyuen）向我方公司 DTDK Co., Ltd 订购如下扫地机器人（robot cleaner）：型号为 6824，数量是 100 台，请写电子邮件婉拒该订单，理由是订货量过小，我方将没有任何利润，请对方加大订购量至 300 件。同时推荐另一种型号为 6820 的扫地机器人，其功能与型号 6824 的机器人类似，因为有现货，所以最小起订量可以是 100 台，其优点是噪音低、吸力强。

Subject	
Content	

Module 6　Dealing with Orders
模块 6　订单处理

Module 7 Payment

模块 ❼
付款

Learning Goals

- Be familiar with typical English term and sentence patterns used in the discussion of international business payment terms with customers.
- Be able to read and write English emails or messages in connection with international business payment.
- Be able to negotiate suitable payment terms with customers.
- Be able to urge the establishment(开立) of Letter of Credit and ask for amendents or extension.

Lead-in

Situation: You're a salesperson. Now your client in Iran asks you whether you can accept D/A 60 days after sight as payment terms during the discussion of export of smartwatch with GPS. However, your company generally only accepts L/C at sight or T/T in advance.

Questions:

1. What would you do before replying to such a request from the customer?
2. How would you respond in the email if you decide to decline such a request?

Introduction

To succeed in today's global marketplace and win sales against competitors, exporters must offer their customers attractive sales terms supported by appropriate payment methods. Because getting paid in full and on time is the ultimate goal for each export sale, an appropriate payment method must be chosen carefully to minimize(最小化) the payment risk while accommodating the needs of the buyer. During or before contract negotiations, we should consider which method is mutually desirable.

Key points to note

- International trade presents a spectrum of risk, which causes uncertainty over the timing of payments between the exporter(seller)and importer(foreign buyer).
- For exporters, any sale has a risk until payment is received. Therefore, exporters want to receive payment as soon as possible, preferably once an order is placed or before the goods are sent to the importer.
- For importers, any payment is a donation until the goods are received. Therefore, importers want to receive the goods as soon as possible but to delay payment as long as possible, preferably until the goods are resold to generate enough income to pay the exporter.

	Least Secure	Less Secure	Medium	More Secure	Most Secure
For Exporter	Consignment（寄售）	Open Account（记账）	Documentary Collections（跟单托收）	Letters of Credit（信用证）	Payment-in-Advance（预付货款）

Payment risk diagram

1. Payment-in-advance（预付货款）

Requiring payment in advance is the least attractive option for the buyer because it creates unfavorable cash flow. Foreign buyers are also concerned that the goods may not be sent if payment is made in advance.

（1）Wire transfer(电汇): the most secure and preferred payment-in-advance method

An international wire transfer is commonly used and is almost immediate. Exporters should provide clear routing instructions to the importer when using this method, including the receiving bank's name and address, SWIFT(Society for Worldwide Interbank Financial Telecommunication)code as well as the seller's name and address, bank account title, and account number. Currently, means of the wire transfer in China's export trade generally include:

T/T Telegraphic Transfer　电汇

Western union　西联汇款

MoneyGram　速汇金

（2）Credit card: a viable cash-in-advance method

Exporters who sell directly to foreign buyers may select credit cards as a viable payment-in-advance option, especially for small consumer-goods transactions.

（3）Escrow service(委托付款服务): a mutually beneficial payment-in-advance method

Escrow in international trade is a service that allows both exporter and importer to protect a transaction by placing the funds in the hands of a trusted third party until a specified set of conditions are met, which are usually in connection with sales in e-commerce platform, such as Amazon, e-Bay, Ali-express, etc.

Here's how it works: the importer sends the agreed amount to the escrow service. After payment is verified, the exporter is instructed to ship the goods. Upon delivery, the importer has a pre-determined amount of time to inspect and accept the goods. Once accepted, the funds are released by the escrow service to the exporter.

2. Letters of credit(信用证)

Letters of credit(L/Cs) are one of the most secure instruments available to international traders. A letter of credit is a commitment by a bank on behalf of the buyer that payment will be made to the exporter, provided that the terms and conditions stated in the L/C have been met, as verified through the presentation of all required documents.

Letter of credit is recommended in higher-risk situations or new or less-established trade relationships. Risk is spread between exporter and importer, provided that all terms and conditions as specified in the L/C are adhered to. However, payment by L/C is a labor intensive process and it is relatively expensive in terms of transaction costs.

3. Documentary collections(跟单托收)

A documentary collection(D/C) is a process in which a seller instructs his bank to forward documents related to the export of goods to a buyer's bank with a request to present these documents to the buyer for a payment, indicating when and on what conditions these documents can be released to the buyer.

(1) Documents against payment(付款交单)

In a D/P collection, the collecting bank releases the documents to the importer only on payment for the goods. Once payment is received, the collecting bank transmits the funds to the remitting bank for payment to the exporter.

(2) Documents against acceptance(承兑交单)

With a D/A collection, the exporter extends credit to the importer by using a time draft. The documents are released to the importer to claim the goods upon his signed acceptance of the time draft.

4. Open account(O/A)(记账)

An open account transaction is a sale where the goods are shipped and delivered before payment is due, which in international sales is typically in 30, 60 or 90 days. This is one of the most advantageous options to the importer in terms of cash flow and cost, but it is consequently one of the riskiest options for an exporter.

5. Consignment(寄售)

Consignment in international trade is a variation of an open account in which payment is sent to the exporter only after the goods have been sold by the foreign distributor to the end customer.

Module 7　Payment
模块 7　付款

Time of payment

Payment before Delivery	Advance payment by T/T, credit card, etc.
Payment against Delivery	● D/P at sight ● L/C
Payment after Delivery	● Open account ● Consignment ● D/A
Installments(分期付款)	Instead of paying all at one time, we can enter the transaction for installment payments. Installment payment terms divide the transaction into multiple payments over a specified period.

Task 1　Negotiating Terms of Payment

In the discussion of international trade, buyers may request easier payment methods, such as O/A or D/A after sight, etc., while sellers tend to use safer payment terms, for instance, L/C at sight or T/T in advance. Therefore, the sellers should handle tactically the buyer's request in terms of payment method.

Section 1　Guidelines

1. Compass

The following are some guidelines on dealing with payment terms.

(1) Evaluate risks, costs and benefits involved

Both parties should assess the risks, cost and benefit involved in connection with the change of payment method. Will it lead to the loss of customers or orders? Will it result in a high risk of payment? How much will it increase or decrease the banking charges or fees?

(2) Refer to your supervisor in case of need

If you cannot decide whether or not to accept the payment method, please refer to your superior for instructions.

(3) Respond to customer's request in a polite way

If you choose to reject a customer's request for the change of payment method, you should reply politely, usually showing a sense of regret, offering a reasonable explanation for the decline, etc.

2. Writing structure

The structure of emails concerning payment terms is as follows.

(1) Propose payment terms
- Refer to the relative product, order or contract.
- Put forward payment terms.
- State the reasons.
- Express hope for acceptance.

(2) Respond to the proposal of payment terms
- Refer to the other party's letter.
- Express agreement or disagreement to his request.
- State the reasons.
- Give a counter-proposal, express hope for acceptance.

Section 2 Samples

Sample 1 propose a payment term

Subject: Our Payment Term with New Customers

Dear Mr. Cooke,

Thank you for your interest in our smartwatches.

About our payment term, our policy with new customers is 30% T/T as down-payment, and 70% T/T against B/L copy.[1]

Attached is our account details for T/T.[2]

We look forward to receiving your first order.

Yours sincerely,
Li Ni(Miss)
3W Co.,Ltd.

Comments

1. 提出付款条件要求。
2. 附上供对方 T/T 转账的相关信息。

Core Vocabulary

T/T(telegraphic transfer)　　　　　电汇

balance	n. 余额
down-payment	n. 预付定金
B/L (bill of lading)	海运提单

Sample 2   ask for a change of payment term

Subject: Payment Terms under S/C No. 20200616

Dear Mr. Zhang,

Regarding your Sales Confirmation Number 20200616 for a power bank in the amount of USD 65 000[1], we would like to propose an easier payment method.

Currently, our purchase from you has been paid by a confirmed, irrevocable letter of credit. But it costs us a great deal and is quite burdensome. From the time L/C is established to the time our domestic buyers pay us, the tie-up of our funds lasts more than three months. Furthermore, bank commission and charges under L/C are expensive in our country, about 2% of the total invoice amount.[2]

Would you please accommodate easier payment terms? We propose D/A 60 days after the B/L date, which would certainly facilitate our business.[3]

We would appreciate your favourable reply.[4]

Best regards,
Bill Bush

Comments

1. 写明订单号或合同号，并表明写信目的。
2. 说明原因。
3. 提出己方的付款方案。
4. 期待对方接受。

Core Vocabulary

tie-up	（资金的）冻结
accommodate	v. 容纳；给……提供方便
burdensome	adj. 麻烦的、累赘的
facilitate	v. 促进，帮助；使容易
establish	v. 开立（信用证）
commission	n. 手续费，佣金

Sample 3 reply to a request to change the payment term

Subject：Payment Terms under S/C No. 20200616

Dear Mr. Bush,

We note from your email that you wish to have a change in payment terms.[1]

We have considered your proposal, but regret to say that at present we have to adhere to our usual practice, that is, payment by confirmed L/C at sight as per our company policy. And we will review your request at the end of this year.[2]

We would appreciate your understanding and cooperation.[3]

Yours faithfully,
Henry Zhang

Comments
1. 简述对方之前的信函内容。
2. 说明不接受对方请求的原因。
3. 期待对方体谅。

Core Vocabulary

adhere to	坚持，追随
policy	政策
as per	按照，依据，如同
review	$v./n.$ 评估

Sample 4 ask for changing a payment method

Subject：Change in Payment Method for New Order

Dear Ms. Wang,

Thanks for the counter-offer for HX-H3 electric bikes on July 15, 2020. We want to place another order with you for 3 000 sets of the bikes, provided that you agree to a change in payment method from L/C at sight to PayPal 10 days before shipment, to reduce the cost of our banking charges & commission.

As we have already established a good business relation with you, your most serious consideration of our request will be appreciated.

We await your positive response.

Yours truly,
Jack White

Core Vocabulary

provided   *conj.* 假如，倘若

Sample 5 respond to request for changing payment term

Subject: Change in Payment Method for New Order

Dear Mr. White,

Thanks for your interest in our HX H3 electric bikes.

As to your request to pay by PayPal 10 days before shipment instead of a letter of credit at sight, please note that we do not usually accept this kind of payment. However, in view of our long-term business relation, we are willing to make an exception for this order.[1]

Please send us the order ASAP so that we can arrange an earlier shipment.[2]

Best Regards,
Mei Wang

Comments

1. 这次接受对方的修改要求，表明此次是破例。
2. 希望对方尽早下订单。

Core Vocabulary

in view of   鉴于；考虑到
make an exception   例外，破例

Section 3 Core Phrases and Sentence Patterns

1. Mention payment terms

- By O/A basis, payment to be made within 60 days after B/L date.
- Payment by L/C draft at 60 days after sight.
- Payment by 60 days sight bill, documents against payment.

- Payment by 180 days date bill, documents against acceptance.
- 70% at sight L/C, 30% T/T(or 80% L/C, 20% T/T, the portion can be negotiated).
- 30% T/T as down-payment, 70% T/T before shipment.
- 30% T/T upon order confirmation as down-payment, 70% L/C at 60 days.
- 50% T/T before shipment, 50% T/T after shipment.
- 40% T/T before shipment, 60% T/T 30 days after B/L date.

2. Propose a payment method

- It would help us greatly if you could accept D/P 30 days after sight.
- Owing to the heavy expense of documentary credit, we suggest that you adopt payment by T/T after goods are ready for shipment.
- Could you please consider an exception and accept payment by D/A 45 days after the B/L date?
- We sincerely hope that you can accommodate us in this respect.

3. Refuse a request regarding the payment method

- We regret that we cannot accept your terms of payment.
- We regret our inability to consider your request for payment under D/A terms.
- As L/C at sight is normal for our export to overseas customers, we can't agree to payment by D/P at sight.
- As we must adhere to our customary practice, we sincerely hope that you will not think us unaccommodating.

4. Accept a request regarding the payment method

- We accept payment on D/P at sight basis for your trial order.
- We understand that you have some difficulties in opening L/C. In view of the small quantity for this order, we accept payment by D/P at sight.
- As a special accommodation, we will accept L/C 60 days after the B/L date for this transaction.
- However, we have to point out that it can't be a precedent (先例) for future business.
- We wish to say that it is in view of our long friendly business relations that we extend you this accommodation.

Task 2

Dealing with Letter of Credit

Letter of credit is a complicated payment method that includes many steps and procedures, such as L/C opening, advising, documents presentation, negotiation, remittance of documents, honor/dishonor of documents, etc. Therefore, mastering the knowledge of L/C is fundamental to the handling of L/C related correspondence.

Section 1 Guidelines

1. Compass

(1) The opening of the letter of credit

The latest arrival time of an L/C usually should be a month before the time of shipment.

The opening time of the L/C is often one of the greatest concerns of the seller. This is because if the seller can receive the L/C at an early stage, he will have time to make enough preparation in the following areas.

- making the goods ready
- booking shipping space
- checking the L/C
- making amendments

(2) Amendments and extension of the letter of credit

L/C is opened against a contract. Upon being accepted, the L/C becomes an independent document and will not be subject to the contract anymore.

The exporter should go through all the clauses in the L/C to make sure they are in full conformity with the terms stipulated in the sales contract.

When there is a delay in shipment, the relevant letter of credit may need to be extended.

2. Writing structure

(1) Urge opening of an L/C

- Referring to the relative order or contract.
- Tell the importer arrangements have been made and that goods will be delivered as soon as the covering L/C comes.
- Ask for an early opening of the L/C(give a deadline if necessary).
- List out some important points agreed upon.

(2) Request L/C amendment

- Express thanks for the opening of the L/C.
- Point out discrepancies(不符合之处)in the L/C with reference to the Contract or Confirmation, or put forward an amendment request and give explanations.
- State desired action(give a deadline if necessary)and wish for a prompt reply.

(3) Request L/C extension

- Express thanks for the opening of the L/C.
- Put forward an extension request and give explanations.
- State desired action and wish a prompt reply.

Section 2　Samples

Sample 1　urge opening of an L/C

Subject: URGENT! Please Open L/C under S/C 20200616 ASAP
Dear Mr. Bush,   Referring to products under our Sales Confirmation No. 20200616[1], we would like to remind you that the delivery date is approaching and we have not yet received the covering L/C.[2]   Please expedite the establishment of the L/C so that we can ship the order on time. Please make sure that the L/C will reach us before <u>November 10, 2020</u>.[3]   To avoid unnecessary amendment, please make sure that the L/C stipulations are in full compliance with the terms of the Sales Confirmation.   We look forward to your early response.   Best regards,   Henry Zhang

Comments
1. 写明订单号或合同号。
2. 提醒对方交货日期临近，我方还没有收到信用证。
3. 敦促对方尽早开立信用证，写明期限。

Core Vocabulary

covering	*adj.* 涵盖的，有关的，项下的
expedite	*v.* 加速
stipulation	*n.* 规定，条文
in compliance with	符合

Sample 2　request amendment of an L/C

Subject: Please Amend L/C. BUA-CFG3869
Dear Mr. White,   We are pleased to receive your L/C No. BUA-CFG3869 under the S/C No. SGM2268.[1]   After carefully checking the terms of L/C with reference to our S/C, we regret to find some discrepancies.

Module 7　Payment
模块 7　付款

(1) The total amount should be **USD 68 300.00**, not USD 63 800.

(2) The Article No. of the payment bar-code scanner should be PBS6280, not PBS6820.

(3) The credit should be available by draft "at sight", not "at 30 days' sight".

(4) The latest shipment date should be August 15, 2022, not August 1, 2022. [2]

We would appreciate it that the amendment to this L/C can reach us before December 25, 2021 , so that shipment can be effected as per S/C terms. [3]

We look forward to your early response.

Kind regards,
Wang Mei

Comments
1. 感谢开立信用证。
2. 指出信用证条款与合同或确认书的不符之处。
3. 提出修改请求，给出修改期限。

Core Vocabulary
discrepancy	n. 不符，矛盾
amendment	n. （信用证）修改

Extended Vocabulary
payment barcode scanner	支付专用的条形码扫描器

Sample 3　seek approval for discrepancies

Subject: Please Accept Discrepancies under L/CBUA-CFG3869

Dear Mr. White,

Please be advised that the following discrepancies under your L/C No. BUA-CFG3869 have been noticed by the negotiating bank (Bank of China Guangzhou Branch).

(1) The shipped on board date is August 16, 2021, while the latest date of shipment in the L/C is August 15, 2021.

(2) The actual port of destination is Dubai, while the port of destination required in the L/C is Kuwait.

As we have obtained your consent on the above issues before shipment, kindly instruct the L/C opening bank to send the acceptance of the above discrepancies to the Bank of China Guangzhou Branch by SWIFT so that we can obtain payment soon.

Best regards,
Wang Mei

Comments

电提不符点,一般是指在信用证支付方式下,受益人提交单据到议付行议付的时候,议付行发现其单据与信用证要求有不相符的地方,即"不符点",那么如果受益人与申请人已经达成一致,可以由开证行授权议付行在存在不符点的情况下做议付。本信就是受益人联系申请人,就不符点进行沟通,要求申请人请求开证行接受不符点。

Core Vocabulary

negotiating bank	议付行
shipped on board	已装船

Extended Vocabulary

SWIFT (society for worldwide interbank financial telecommunications)　环球同业银行金融电讯协会

Sample 4　ask to extend an L/C

Subject: Pls Extend L/C BUA-CFG3869 to September 30

Dear Mr. White,

We regret to say that despite our effort, we cannot guarantee shipment by the agreed date due to the delay in raw material supplies. We are worried that your L/C may expire before shipment. Would you please kindly extend the expiry date to September 30, 2021?

We're sorry for this delay, and will be grateful for your understanding.

Best regards,
Wang Mei

Core Vocabulary

in spite of	尽管
raw material	原材料
be grateful for sth	对……表示感激

Section 3 Core Phrases and Sentence Patterns

1. Urging opening of L/C

- Please open the relevant L/C in time so that we can deliver goods as per the stipulations in the contract.
- We wish to make it clear that L/C should reach us before August 1, 2020, otherwise we may not be able to effect shipment in time.
- We would be grateful if you could expedite the opening of L/C to ensure the fulfillment of the contract.
- The S/C stipulates that shipment must be effected before September 30 and L/C should reach us by the end of July. However, until now we have not received your L/C. Please kindly open L/C as agreed ASAP.

2. Asking for the amendment of L/C

- We find that both the latest date of shipment and expiry date should be extended by 30 days respectively.
- The following 3 points do not conform to the contract and should thus be amended.
- We found that the amount of your L/C is insufficient. Please rush the amendment and increase the amount to $1 560.
- Please amend the covering L/C to allow transshipment and partial shipment.
- After checking the L/C, we request you to make the following amendments.

(1) The quantity should read: 1 000 M/Ts(5% more or less, at seller's option).

(2) ...

Task 3

Settling Other Payment Problems

In international business, there are various kinds of payment-related problems. In the first place, overdue payments can cause chaos for businesses, especially for small businesses. If our incoming cash is intermittent(断断续续的) and unpredictable, it's much harder to manage our outgoing cash. Organizing and polishing our overdue payment reminder communications is critical to having a functional collection process.

Section 1 Guidelines

One of the best things we can do to encourage our clients to pay on time is to communicate with them regularly via an organized set of payment reminder emails.

We need to modulate our tone across the reminder emails. We need to be polite and firm—but, if the payment is getting very late, our tone need to get harsher.

In addition, the email should include the following parts.

- A clear call to action
- Emphasis on how long the payment is overdue
- A copy of the invoice in the attachment

Section 2 Samples

Sample 1   send bank account information

Subject: Our Bank Account Info. for L/C under S/C 20200616

Dear Mr. Bush,

Below is our bank account information. Please kindly remit funds under S/C No. 202207368 to us accordingly.

BENEFICIARY: Guangzhou Good luck Co. Ltd

BANK ACCOUNT NO.: 236-862392

BENEFICIARY BANK NAME: Agricultural bank of China, Guangzhou Branch

SWIFT CODE: ABOCCNBJ190

Best regards,
Henry Zhang

Core Vocabulary

remit	v.	汇款，汇寄
fund	n.	资金；v. 投资，资助
beneficiary	n.	受益人

Module 7　Payment
模块 7　付款

Sample 2　urge settlement of an overdue payment

Subject: Invoice #10237 is One Week Overdue

Hi Mr. Bush,

Our records show that we haven't yet received payment of $5 400 for Invoice #10237, which is overdue by one week. As your payments to us have always been on time, I wonder what goes wrong this time. Please check this out on your end.[1]

Attached is the invoice with the amount due. Please make the payment ASAP.[2]

Thanks,
Henry

Comments

1. 在催促客户之前，先询问客户原因。前一两次催款，可以写得简短、语气委婉，如本封邮件提到过去买家总是准时付款，在催款同时为买家保留面子。
2. 写清楚希望对方采取什么行动，即尽早付款。

Core Vocabulary

overdue	*adj.* （到期）未付的，未还的，过期的
check sth. out	调查
on one's end	在某人一方

Sample 3　another email to urge payment

Email subject: Invoice #10237 from 3/25 is Overdue—Please Send Payment ASAP

Hi Mr. Bush,

This is another reminder that I have yet to receive the $5 400 owed on invoice #10237.

Please be aware that, as per my terms, I may charge you an additional interest on payment received more than 30 days past its due date.

Again, please reach out if you have any questions about this payment. Otherwise, please arrange a settlement of this invoice immediately.

Kind regards,
Henry

Comments

第二次、第三次催款表达要更加直接，语气更加强硬，但仍然保持专业和友好的姿态。

Core Vocabulary

reminder	n. 提醒
reach out	联系
interest	n. 利息
settlement	n. 清偿，结清

Sample 4　urge overdue payment under D/A

Subject: USD56 200 Overdue

Dear Mr. White,

Please note that the draft of USD56 200 under invoice No. 3862 is now 30 days overdue, which was sent to you on May 10, 2020 based on D/A 60 days after the B/L date.

Although we have contacted you several times for the payment, so far we still have not received any answer from you.

Please effect payment to us without further delay to avoid putting your credit in jeopardy. We will be forced to take legal measures to collect the funds if no response from you before Sept. 30, 2020.

Regards,
Wang Mei

Comments

本催款邮件写得比较严厉，它指出经与对方多次联系，仍未得到答复，因此声明如果对方仍不回复，会采取法律途径处理。这种是卖家估计买家已经不太可能在友好洽谈的情况下付款而采用的对买家的警告。

Core Vocabulary

draft	n. 汇票
D/A 60 days after B/L date	承兑交单；提单日后60天付款
jeopardy	n. 危险
legal measures	法律措施

Section 3　Core Phrases and Sentence Patterns

(1) This is just to remind you that payment on invoice ♯10237, which we sent on March 25th, will be due next week.

(2) We regret to advise that invoice ♯10237 is now 14 days overdue.

(3) If you need any further information or documentation to pay this invoice, please let me know.

(4) Please advise us of the status of this payment as it is now more than 14 days overdue.

(5) Further to my previous correspondence, I'm contacting you once again with regard to the outstanding invoice ♯10237.

(6) Could you please let me know when we can expect payment?

(7) If payment has already been made, please disregard this email.

(8) We require immediate settlement of this payment to avoid further action.

(9) Given the lack of response on your side after several attempts to contact you, we will shortly begin legal proceedings in order to receive the money owed to us.

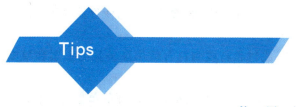

信 用 证

信用证是指银行根据进口人（买方）的请求，开给出口人（卖方）的一种保证承担支付货款责任的书面凭证。在信用证内，银行授权出口人在符合信用证所规定的条件下，以该行或其指定的银行为付款人，开具不得超过规定金额的汇票，并按规定随附装运单据，按期在指定地点收取货款。

信用证的当事人主要有以下类型。

（1）开证申请人（applicant），向银行申请开立信用证的人，在信用证中又称开证人（opener）。

（2）开证银行（opening/issuing bank），是指应开证申请人的要求开立信用证的银行，一般为进口商所在地银行。开证银行应根据开证申请人的要求，及时、正确地开立信用证。信用证开立之后，开证银行便承担凭单付款的责任，而不管进口商是否拒绝赎单或无力支付。

（3）受益人（beneficiary），是指信用证上明确指定并由其接受信用证，凭发票（invoice）、提单（bill of lading）等收取货款的人，即出口商。受益人接受信用证后，应按信用证有关条款的规定，装运货物，提交单据，据以收取货款。

（4）付款银行（paying bank），是指信用证上指定的信用证项下汇票的付款的，一般为开证银行，也可以是开证银行指定的另一家银行。

（5）议付银行（negotiating bank），是指在议付类型信用证中，愿意按照信用证上的指示，买入受益人交来的跟单汇票的银行，它可以根据信用证上的相关条款及有关指示将相关单据寄给开证银行,向开证银行索回所垫货款。

(6) 通知银行(advising bank),是指接受开证银行委托将信用证通知给出口商的银行,一般为出口商所在银行,只负责证明信用证的真实性,不承担其他义务。

(7) 保兑行(confirming bank),受开证行委托对信用证以自己名义保证付款的银行。

常见信用证有以下种类。

(1) 跟单信用证(documentary credit),是凭跟单汇票或仅凭单据付款的信用证。国际贸易结算中所使用的信用证绝大部分是跟单信用证。

(2) 光票信用证(clean letter of credit),是凭不附带单据的汇票付款的信用证。

(3) 可撤销信用证(revocable letter of credit),是指开证行对所开信用证不必征得受益人同意有权随时撤销的信用证。实际应用中已经很少见到此类信用证。

(4) 不可撤销信用证(irrevocable letter of credit),是指信用证一经开出,在有效期内,非经信用证各有关当事人的同意,开证行不能片面修改或撤销的信用证。此种信用证在国际贸易中使用得多。

(5) 保兑信用证(confirmed letter of credit),是指经开证行以外的另一家银行加具保兑的信用证。保兑信用证主要是受益人(出口商)对开证银行的资信不了解,对开证银行的国家政局、外汇管制过于担心,怕收不回货款而要求加具保兑的要求,从而使货款的回收得到双重保障。

(6) 即期信用证(sight credit),是开证行或付款行收到符合信用证条款的汇票和单据后,立即履行付款义务的信用证。

(7) 远期信用证(usance credit),是开证行或付款行收到符合信用证的单据时,不立即付款,而是等到汇票到期才履行付款义务的信用证。

Communication Laboratory

I. Fill in each of the following blanks with a proper word/words given in the box. Change the form if necessary.

discrepancy	extend	overdue	regret
confirmed	expedite	amend	irrevocable

1. The following 3 points do not conform to the contract and should thus be _____.
2. We _____ our inability to accept your request for payment by D/P 60 days after sight.
3. We would be grateful if you could _____ the establishment of L/C to ensure the fulfillment of the contract.
4. After checking the L/C, we found some _____, which should be amended by

Module 7　Payment
模块 7　付款

the issuing bank so that we can go ahead to execute the contract.

5．Please note that the draft of USD 56 200 under invoice No. 3862 is now 30 days _____．

6．We are afraid that your L/C will expire before shipment. Please kindly _____ the expiry date to July 30, 2021．

II. Translate the following sentences into English.

1．我们已经认真考虑了贵方的建议，但非常遗憾，目前我们不得不按照我们公司的政策，采用保兑的即期信用证付款。

2．请注意我们通常不接受付款交单这种付款方式。然而，考虑到我们长期的业务关系，我们愿意在这次订货时破例采用。

3．关于2820号销售确认书项下的商品，装运日期已临近，但我们至今仍未收到贵方的有关信用证。

4．为避免随后的修改，请确保信用证规定与销售合同的条款完全一致。

5．为确保合同能够准时执行，请尽快安排开立信用证。希望信用证能在2020年8月15日之前到达我方。

6．在仔细检查贵方开来的信用证后，我们遗憾地发现一些不符点，需要贵方指示开证行进行相应的修改。

7．请把信用证的装船期和有效期分别延长至2020年9月30日和2020年10月21日。

8．在此通知贵方，发票号13692项下的9 600美元现已逾期15天。

III. Write an email in English based on the situation given.

1．我方公司名字为GZKA Co., Ltd., 向埃及ALABA Co., Ltd. (联系人：Abdul Aziz) 出口运动手环。对方考虑到信用证手续费太贵，手续烦琐，而且周转时间长，发来电子邮件商量改用预付货款15%，剩余货款用即期付款交单支付。请回信协商，提出T/T预付款30%，剩余货款凭提单副本(B/L copy)T/T支付。

2. 我方公司名字为GZKA Co.,Ltd.,向埃及ALABA Co.,Ltd.（联系人：Abdul Aziz）出口运动手环，发现对方开来的信用证中存在以下问题：信用证的货物型号错了，不应是SB3686，而应该是SB3886；信用证应该是即期付款，而不是30 days after sight；应该是允许分批装运的，而不是禁止分批装运。请写邮件联系对方修改信用证。

3. 我方公司名字为GZKA Co.,Ltd.,向埃及ALABA Co.,Ltd.（联系人：Abdul Aziz）出口电动单车，发现对方有一笔货款USD9 800（发票号码WR368622项下）未付款，已经过期两周。请写邮件联系对方立刻付款。

Module 8 Packing, Shipment and Insurance

Learning Goals

- ❖ Know about the key points of business correspondence concerning packing, shipment and insurance.
- ❖ Be familiar with typical words, expressions and sentence patterns useful for business correspondence concerning packing, shipment and insurance.
- ❖ Be able to write effective and professional business letters concerning packing, shipment and insurance.

Lead-in

Situation: After the order is confirmed, you need to prepare for production. You are required to deal with correspondence about packing requirements and do the packing properly. Also, you need to arrange shipment and insurance.

Questions:

1. What types of packing are there? And what functions do they serve?
2. What are shipping documents? Could you name some of them?
3. How to arrange a shipment in international business?
4. If you receive an email from your client asking to cover additional risks, how would you reply?

Task 1

Writing on Packing Requirements

Packing plays a very important role in international business. It can protect goods and keep them good and complete as they are shipped. In addition, packing can provide information about goods such as name, origin, specification, weight, quantity, etc, which can make customers convenient for selecting, carrying and using goods. Nowadays, the significance of packing has increasingly been recognized and more and more attention has been paid to it. When talking about packing here, we usually refer to transportation packing, the outer packing of the goods.

Section 1　Guidelines

As for packing, details such as the manner of packing, kinds of packing materials, marking on the packing, the burden of packing cost, etc. should be involved.

1. Compass

(1) Kinds of packing

There are two forms of packing: outer packing for transportation and inner packing for sales.

Outer packing is used mainly to keep the goods safe and sound during transportation. Outer packing includes cases, bales, barrels, bags, baskets, pallets, containers and so on. It must be not only solid enough to prevent the packed goods from any damage but also provide easy marks for operation staff at the docks to distinguish the goods they handle and for consignees to identify their goods when receiving at the destination ports.

Inner packing is not only designed to protect goods but also to help customers identify goods, make goods appealing to customers, publicize the goods and promote sales. It is an essential promotional tool for the sale of products.

(2) Packing marks

Packing marks are integral to packing. It refers to different diagrams, words and figures that are written, printed or brushed on the outside of transportation packing. There are three kinds of packing marks: shipping marks, indicative marks and warning marks.

① Shipping marks

Shipping marks are used for the identification of shipments during transit to ensure smooth and prompt delivery. They are not only stenciled on the transportation packing of cargoes but also appear on documents such as invoices, insurance policy or certificates, bills of lading, etc.

② Indicative marks

Indicative mark refers to the symbols or words that indicate the nature of the contents of the package and give instructions to facilitate the smooth handling of the cargo that needs special care. Indicative marks are usually comprised of noticeable designs, remarkable diagrams and simple words or numbers on the package such as "HANDLE WITH CARE" "THIS SIDE UP" "NO HOOK", etc. Here are some examples.

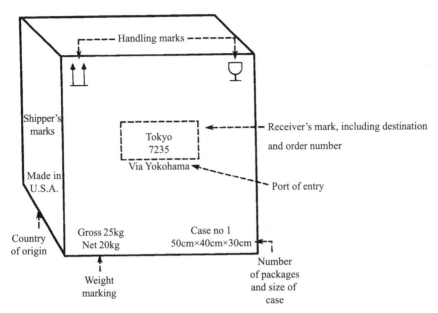

Shipping marks

Indicative marks

③ Warning marks

A warning mark is used to indicate dangerous cargoes and is suitable to remind people that the cargo is explosive, inflammable, poisonous, corrosive, radioactive, etc. It tells people to take safety measures to avoid any possible harm and damage when they handle the goods.

Warning marks

(3) Packing clause

The packing clause is one of the main conditions in a sales contract and also an integral part of a sales contract or a letter of credit. The general packing clauses are as follows.

① The packing materials: cases, bales, barrels, drums, containers, etc.

② The packing specification: quantity in each unit, dimension in each package, etc.

③ The packing cost: who is to bear the packing cost, the seller or the buyer.

④ The packing marks: shipping marks, indicative marks and warning marks.

(4) Packing list

A packing list is often one of the required documents that the exporter should submit to the bank for negotiation under the payment method of L/C. From the list, the buyer and the carrier can determine how many packages there should be and the particular items in each one. It is a kind of confirmation of the detailed information of the shipment of cargo exported.

2. Writing structure

(1) Writing to instruct packing requirements(from the importer to the exporter)

- Refer to the relative order or contract and state the purpose of writing.
- Make clear requirements for packing.
- Put forward suggestions if any.
- Express thanks and ask for a favorable reply.

(2) Responding to the importer's packing requirements(from the exporter to the importer)

- Identify the reference number and state the topic.
- State and confirm the packing requirements or details.
- Express expectation.

Section 2 Samples

Sample 1 packing instruction

Subject: Packing Instruction for Order No. ET-648

Dear Cindy,

Thanks for your email of January 17.

Attached is Order No. ET-648 for 3 000 pieces of electronic toys. As this is the first transaction between us, we are writing you to make clear packing requirements for the contracted goods.

All items are to be packed in poly bags of one piece each and then to a box, 12 boxes to a carton lined with waterproof and shake-proof material. Please see to it that the cartons should be strong enough to protect the goods from any possible damage in transit. Shipping marks to be stenciled in a diamond to the outer packing are indicated as follows.

Module 8　Packing, Shipment and Insurance
模块 8　包装、装运和保险

Indicative marks such as "KEEP DRY" "Open here" and warning marks as "Inflammable" should appear on the outer packing to avoid any negligence that may cause unexpected trouble and expenses.

ASSRD
ET-648
NEW YORK
N0.1-30

We trust that you can meet the above requirements and thanks for your cooperation.

Yours sincerely,
Robert

Core Vocabulary

transaction	*n.* 交易
line	给（衣服、箱子等）装衬里
in transit	运送中的，运输途中的
shipping marks	装运指示
indicative marks	指示性标志
warning marks	警告性标志
negligence	*n.* 忽略，忽视

Extended Vocabulary

stencil	*n./v.* （印刷图案或文字的）模板
inflammable	*adj.* 易燃的

Sample 2　packing instruction

Subject: Re: Packing Instruction for Order No. ET-648

Dear Mr. Robert,

Thanks for your email of January 19, in which you put forward some requirements for package and marking on the contracted goods. We are writing to inform you that we would have the goods packed as requested.

Our packing with cartons for electronic toys has been widely accepted by our customers. The cartons are lined with foam plastics to protect the goods against the press. We have especially reinforced our packing with straps outside to reduce any possible damage in transit. Besides, they will be carried in containers, which may greatly reduce the chance of pilferage and damage caused by rough handling. The destination port and order number have been marked and such indicative marks as "KEEP DRY" as well as warning marks as "INFLAMMABLE" have been stenciled.

If you think this is acceptable to you, please let us know as soon as possible.

Yours faithfully,
Cindy

Core Vocabulary

put forward	提出
foam plastic	泡沫塑料
reinforce	v. 加强,加固
strap	n. 皮带,带条;v. 用带捆绑
rough handling	粗暴处理

Extended Vocabulary

pilferage	n. 偷窃,行窃

Sample 3   advise a client of packing details

Subject: Packing for Fragile Goods

Dear Michael,

Thanks for your email of June 2, requesting the packing plan in detail for our Chinese teacup.

Please rest assured that we have always paid particular attention to the safety of packing fragile goods. Each teacup is wrapped in tissue paper and in an individual cardboard box. Then we pack the boxes into strong cartons, 12 to a carton, separated from each other by corrugated paper dividers. Such warnings like "USE NO HOOK" "OPEN HERE" "DON'T DROP" will be written on the case.

The packages are not only shock-proof but also damp-proof. For years we have used these packages in our shipments to many continental ports.

We hope this has made you doubly assured.

Looking forward to receiving your order soon.

Yours faithfully,
Tim

Core Vocabulary

fragile goods	易碎物品
wrap	*v.* 包,缠绕,包起来
tissue paper	棉纸,薄纸
individual	*adj.* 单独的,独个的
shock-proof	*adj.* 抗震的,防震的,抗冲击的
damp-proof	*adj.* 防潮的,防湿的

Extended Vocabulary

divider	*n.* 分隔物	corrugated paper	瓦楞纸,波状纸板

Section 3　Core Phrases and Sentence Patterns

1. Talk about packing requirements and details

（1）包装容器名称

英文	中文	英文	中文	英文	中文
bag	袋	carton	纸板箱	barrel	琵琶桶
bale	包、布包	crate	板条箱	poly-bag	塑料袋
bundle	捆	pallet	托盘	tin, can	罐头
gunny bag	麻袋	drum	铁皮圆桶	containers	集装箱
case	箱	packet	小包装纸袋、小硬纸板盒	sack	麻布(或厚纸、塑料等)大袋

（2）描述包装的防护效果

防潮	damp-proof	防湿	moisture-proof
防震	shock-proof	经受得住长期海运	can withstand long sea voyage
防漏	leakage-proof	经受得住颠簸	can withstand bumping
防水	water-proof	经受得住粗暴搬运	can withstand rough handling
防锈	rust-proof	耐震动,耐摇晃	pack against jolting

（3）集装箱的相关缩写

LCL	Less Than Container Load	拼箱
FCL	Full Container Load	整柜
GP	General Purpose	通用集装箱,指标准高度的集装箱,高度2 591mm
HC	High Cubic	高柜,指高度较高的集装箱,高度为2 896mm
TEU	Twenty Feet Equivalent Units	20英尺标准集装箱
FEU	Forty Feet Equivalent Units	40英尺标准集装箱

（4）（货物）包装在……（纸箱、袋子、木箱、布包、盒子、麻袋、板条箱、桶、罐头、捆等）里：be packed in…；have sth. packed in…；be wrapped in…；be wrapped with…

- We wish to have the ear-plugs packed one piece in a poly-bag, 20 pieces to a carton, and 100 cartons total in an FCL.
- Leggings（紧身裤）are to be packed in wooden cases of 10 dozens each.
- Slippers（拖鞋）are to be packed in wooden cases, each containing 50 dozens.

（5）内衬……、有……内衬：be lined/padded with…；have an inner lining/padding of…；with…liner

用……加固：be secured with/by…；be reinforced by…；be mounted with…；be bound with…

- Each crate is padded with waterproof material and bound with hard straps thus preventing the goods from moisture and damage in transit.
- Each case is lined with foam plastics to protect the goods against the press.
- We have especially reinforced our packing with double straps to minimize the extent of any possible damage to the goods.

（6）提及印制在包装上的相关标志：be printed on…；be stenciled on…；be marked…

- Indicative marks such as "Handle with care" and warning marks as "Corrosive" "Poisonous" should be printed on the package.
- The glassware needs special packing against jolting and the surface of each outer package should be marked "Fragile".

2. Reply to packing requirements and mention packing details

- Many thanks for your email of December 22 concerning packing requirements for goods under S/C No. BR 756, and we will make an immediate arrangement accordingly.
- Taking into consideration the transport at your end, we have especially reinforced our packing and lined the goods with polythene.
- All the goods have been wrapped with soft paper, padded with the poly membrane inside, mounted with iron belts externally and packed with a wooden pallet.
- As requested, the goods have been packed in plastic bags, strapped by three woven belts outside and shipped in containers, 20 bags for each.
- We have strictly followed your instructions to pack the goods and you can be assured that they will reach you smoothly and safely.
- We can meet your requirements to have the goods packed in wooden cases but the extra packing charges will be for your account.
- Thanks for your packing guidance, but it is regretful that we cannot meet your request for using special packing materials.

3. Express thanks and ask for a favorable reply

- Please send us the shipping advice promptly. Awaiting your early reply.
- We hope the goods will reach you in perfect condition. Looking forward to your favorable news.

Writing on Shipment Arrangement

Delivering goods to the buyer is one of the seller's major obligations（职责）under the sales contract. The seller should fulfill the obligation quickly, carefully and economically. The main activities include custom clearance（清关）, vessel chartering（船舶租赁）or shipping space booking, obtaining shipping documents after passing goods to the shipping company, and sending shipping advice. Goods can be transported by road, rail or air, but in most cases of international trade, by sea. We will focus on the most common conveyance method—ocean transportation.

Section 1 Guidelines

1. Compass

According to the usual practice, after a contract is confirmed, it is the exporter's duty to prepare goods for shipment and book shipping space under the terms of CIF or CFR while on the FOB basis this will be arranged by the importer.

(1) Method of shipment

In international trade, shipment can be made by sea, air, rail, truck and parcel. In order to deliver the goods more efficiently, we also have multimode transport（多式联运）and land bridge transport（陆桥运输）. The choice of shipping methods depends on the nature of the products, the distance to be shipped, available means of transportation, and relative freight costs.

(2) Terms of shipment

Time of shipment

- Shipment during October.
- Shipment before December 30.
- Shipment within 30 days after receipt of the relevant L/C.

Port of shipment and port of destination

The port of shipment and the port of destination is related to the trade terms, they may be stipulated in the following ways.

- FOB Shenzhen and Guangzhou, China.
- CIF New York.
- CIF London, optional Hamburg/Rotterdam; Optional charges for the buyer's account.

Partial shipment（分批装运）

- Partial shipments allowed (prohibited).
- Ship half of the order in April and the balance one month later.

- Shipment to be spread over 3 months, beginning from September.
- Shipment should be effected within March/April/May in three lots.

Transshipment（转运）
- Transshipment allowed/permitted.
- Transshipment prohibited.
- Transshipment allowed at Hong Kong.

（3）Shipping documents（船运单据）

Shipping documents are legal documents that are utilized in the process of transporting goods from one location to another. Shipping documents are important to protect all parties involved in the shipping process. By complying with the shipping regulations, it is possible to ensure that orders are correct, delivered on time, packaged in a manner that is in keeping with shipping standards, and that the rates charged for the shipping process itself are compatible with any contracts that exist between the shipper and the carrier. International trade attaches great importance to shipping documents. Generally, shipping documents contain the following documents.

commercial invoice	商业发票	weight memo	重量单
insurance policy	保险单	certificate of origin	原产地证明
bill of lading	提单	certificate of inspection	检验证书
packing list	装箱单		

（4）Shipping instruction（装运指示）

Shipping instruction is a written document which states, other than what has been regulated in the sales contract or the letter of credit, the packing requirements and shipping marks of the cargo. Before shipment, the importer usually sends the shipping requirements to the exporter, informing him of the packing, shipping marks and mode of transport, etc. Such a notice is called shipping instruction.

（5）Shipping advice（装船通知）

After the goods are loaded on board for shipment, the exporter should promptly inform the importer of the details of the shipment so that the importer can make preparation for receiving the goods and considering the sales distribution channels and more urgently, effect insurance if the trade term is FOB or CFR. Such a notice is called shipping advice.

（6）Notice of cargo readiness（货物准备就绪的通知）

Under FOB terms, when the goods are ready for shipment, the exporter should, within a reasonable period, send the importer by email a "…days'(definite) notice of cargo readiness" in order to leave ample time for the importer to charter a ship or book shipping space and arrange insurance.

（7）Bill of lading（提单）

A bill of lading is a type of document that is used to acknowledge the receipt of a shipment of goods. A transportation company or carrier typically issues this document to a shipper. In addition the document indicates the particular vessel on which the goods have been placed, their intended destination and the terms for transporting the shipment to its final destination. It also includes a description of the goods that are being shipped, their weight and other shipping details. It is the cargo receipt, the evidence of the carriage contract, and most importantly, the document of title(or ownership)to the goods.

2. Writing structure

(1) Advise shipment information and send shipping advice

- Refer to the relative order or contract and state the purpose of writing.
- State shipping information.
- Present shipping documents.
- Express your expectation and ask for a favorable reply.

(2) Request prompt shipment

- Express your thanks for the in-coming letter and state the purpose of writing.
- State reasons for urging shipment.
- State consequences for delayed delivery.
- Express your expectation and ask for a favorable reply.

(3) Reply to prompt shipment request

- Express your thanks for the in-coming letter and state the purpose of writing.
- Express your regret for the delayed shipment and state reasons.
- State the actions taken and shipment arrangement.
- Express your expectation of understanding and cooperation.

Section 2 Samples

Sample 1 urge prompt shipment

Subject: Pls Ship Order No. ET-648 Immediately

Dear Cindy,

Regarding our Order No. ET-648 covering 3 000 pieces of electronic toys, we sent to you about 15 days ago an irrevocable L/C expiring till December 2. However, up to now, we have not received from you any information.

As the Christmas season is approaching, our customers are badly in need of the goods. Please rush shipment as soon as possible. We must insist on immediate delivery. Otherwise, we shall be compelled to cancel the order according to the stipulations in the contract.

We hope to receive your shipping advice soon.

Yours sincerely,
Robert

Comments

按 CIF、CFR 价成交,由卖方租船,在装运期限将至,而卖方仍未发出装船通知的情况下,买方则会发函敦促卖方按照信用证或合同的规定准时交货。按 FOB 价成交,则由买方派船,当装运期已到,而卖方仍未收到买方派船的消息,也会发函敦促买方按照信用证或合同的规定准时派船。

Core Vocabulary

expire	v. 失效,终止
compel	v. 被迫,迫使

Sample 2　reply to a shipment request

Subject: Update on the Shipment of Order No. ET-648

Dear Mr. Robert,

We have received your email requesting us to expedite the shipment of your order No. ET-648.[1]

We are sorry for the inconvenience. A recent typhoon hit our city and damaged our workshops, which brought a standstill of work for five days. Luckily, our production is back to normal now. We assure you that we will load the goods without any delay.[2]

You may receive our shipping advice <u>before October 25, 2021</u>.[3] I hope the goods will reach you in sound condition and that you will find our goods satisfactory.

We appreciate your understanding and cooperation.

Yours sincerely,
Cindy

Comments

1. 确认收到对方的来信。
2. 解释交货延迟的原因,提出解决方案。
3. 告知对方下一步的动作。

Core Vocabulary

workshop	*n.* 工厂,车间
standstill	*n.* 停止,停顿
in sound condition	状况良好

Sample 3   reply to a shipment request

Subject: An Update on Your Order #12756

Hi Rhonda,

It's Patrick here. I wanted to reach out on behalf of DOTTA to sincerely apologize for the delay in shipment of your Order #12756. [1]

We're experiencing a higher than usual demand for our scooters this month and your order was unfortunately delayed. We are doing everything we can to get your much-needed scooters to you by the end of October. [2]

To further show our sincere apology, please accept this gift with your next order. Just click the link below. [3]

Click here to claim your free gift→

Again, I apologize for the delay and appreciate your understanding. [4]

Thank you for choosing DOTTA.

Patrick
Sales Manager
DOTTA Intelligent Technology

Comments

1. 真诚道歉。
2. 解释原因,并给出解决方案,最好能明确回答对方最关心的问题,如什么时候之前能交货。
3. 提出补偿,这里是下次下单时将送礼品。
4. 表达希望得到对方理解,并再次道歉。

Sample 4　send shipping advice

Subject：Shipping Advice for Order ET-648

Dear Mr. Robert,

We are pleased to inform you that your Order ET-648 for 3 000 pieces of electronic toys has been shipped via S. S. "FLOWER" today. All items were examined before being packed in containers. You may rest assured that they should reach you in good condition by <u>the middle of December</u>.

We have sent you via DHL one set of shipping documents so that you may make all the necessary preparations to take delivery of the goods when they arrive at your port.

　　（1）Invoice No. 4156 in duplicate.
　　（2）Packing list N0. 8123 in duplicate.
　　（3）One Copy of Non-negotiable Bill of Lading No. AD157.
　　（4）One copy of the Insurance Policy No. DB689.
　　（5）One copy of the Survey Report No. RT3671.

I am sure you will find the shipment satisfactory. We look forward to more opportunities of serving you.

Yours sincerely,
Cindy

Comments

装船通知可分为未装船通知和已装船通知。未装船通知是在收到订舱确认书之后发出的，告知船名及船次、预计开船时间（ETD）、预计到达时间（ETA）、当地船务代理等信息。已装船通知是货物已实际上船后发出，其内容基本一致。

按照FOB或CFR价成交，卖方在装船前应及时通知买方，以便买方及时对货物进行投保。由于通知不及时而出现的损失由卖方承担。

按FOB成交，由买方负责租船。在预计的装船时间前应通知卖方，发出装船指示（shipping instruction）。装船指示信函内容与装船通知内容大致相同，有时也可以增加对包装、保险等的要求。

Core Vocabulary

in duplicate	一式两份
Non-negotiable Bill of Lading	不可转让提单
Insurance Policy	保险单

Module 8　Packing, Shipment and Insurance
模块 8　包装、装运和保险

Sample 5　send shipping advice

Subject: ETA for Order #ET-780

Dear Alison,

The goods of Order #ET-780 were shipped by S. S. SHUN FENG. Attached are the loading photos of the cargo for your reference.

Please also find the following.
  (1) Invoice No. 718.
  (2) Telex Release B/L No. AD256.

The ship date was September 20, and the ETA is about November 12.

Best regards,
Cindy

Extended Vocabulary

ETA (estimated time of arrival)　预计抵达时间

Telex Release B/L　电放提单（电报放货的简称，是通过电子报文或者电子信息形式把提单信息发送至目的港船公司。收货人可凭加盖电放章的提单电放件和电放保函进行换单提货。）

Section 3　Core Phrases and Sentence Patterns

1. Urge for prompt shipment
- As the season is rapidly approaching, our buyers are badly in need of the goods.
- As the contracted time of delivery is rapidly falling due, you must inform us of the delivery time without any further delay.
- Hope that you could ship the goods by the next steamer "Diamond" which is due to sail from your city on or about the 15 July to our port, as our clients are anxious to have these goods within the next month.

2. Advice information about the shipment
- We would like to inform you that the goods were already shipped out on September 10.
- We have shipped you today by S. S. "DAWU" 400 cartons of notebooks. They are to be transshipped to Shanghai and are expected to reach your port in the middle of this month.
- Pleased to say that we have shipped the goods by "Dongfeng" which left Shanghai today.

● Glad to tell you that today we have shipped the goods under your Order No. 478 onboard S. S "LIGHT" which will sail for your port tomorrow.

外贸货物的包装

1. 包装条款

合同中包装条款通常包括包装材料,包装方式的规定,包装标志和包装费等。值得注意的是,在实际操作中要考虑商品特点和不同运输方式的要求,对包装规定要明确具体,明确包装由谁供应和包装费由谁负担。包装的供应一般有以下三种。

(1) 由卖方供应包装,包装连同商品一起交付买方。

(2) 由卖方供应包装,交货后,卖方将原包装收回。对原包装返回卖方的运费由谁负担,应作具体规定。

(3) 由买方供应包装或包装材料,应规定如包装或包装材料未能及时提供影响发运时,买卖双方所负的责任。

2. 货物运输的流程

出口商(exporter),通常是发货方(consignor)必须知道所载货物的船名和船只起航日期。收到信用证后,必须立即与船公司(shipping company)或者货运代理(shipping agents)联系订舱,按照进口商的装船须知(importer's shipping instruction)准备装运。其中装船须知一般已在签订的货物合同中体现。货物装船后,船主或者货运代理将立刻开出一张所载货物的收据,即提单(bill of lading),正本提单一般一式三份。出口商把提单连同发票和其他装船单据送交银行以议付开给开证行的汇票。与此同时,出口商发出装船通知,将船名、起航日期及其他装船细节告知进口商。

3. 货物装运通知

货物装运通知也称装船通知,其作用是让进口商做好资金筹措、付款和接货准备。如果成交条件是 FOB/FCA、CFR/CPT 等,还需要向进口国保险公司发出该通知,以便其为进口商办理货物保险事项。装船通知的主要内容如下。

(1) 单据名称。主要为 Shipping/Shipment Advice、Advice of Shipment 等,也有人称之为 shipping statement/declaration。

(2) 通知内容。主要包括所运货物的合同号或信用证号、品名、数量、金额、运输工具名称、起航时间、起运地点和目的地、提单号码、运输标志等相关细节,这些信息要与其他的相关单据保持一致。

(3) 制作和发出日期。日期不能超过信用证规定的发出日期,否则为违约。常见的有以小时为准(within 24/48 hours)和以天为准(within 2 days after shipment date)。若信用证上没有明确规定,应在装船后尽快发出此通知,如果信用证规定"Immediately after shipment"(装船后立即通知),应控制在提单后三天之内发出。

Module 8 Packing, Shipment and Insurance
模块 8 包装、装运和保险

Writing on Insurance Arrangement

Section 1 Guidelines

1. Compass

Insurance is a very important aspect of foreign trade business. During the long-distance carriage of goods from the seller to the buyer by land, by air or by sea, it is inevitable to encounter different kinds of unexpected accidents or perils and possibly suffer losses. It is necessary to apply to an insurance company before the transit.

Key concepts related to insurance as follows.

underwriter	保险商	insurer	保险人,承保人
insurance applicant	投保人	insurant, the insured	被保险人,受保人
insured amount	保险金额	risk	险别
insurance clause	保险条款	coverage	保险范围
premium	保险费	premium rate	保险费率

Here are three points to consider when securing air or marine insurance.

(1) Get enough coverage. Many people ask for coverage in the amount of 110% of their transaction value, including freight costs and insurance. The extra 10% is to compensate for lost time, profits, and any legal or other expenses. The premium is calculated according to the risks involved. A policy that protects against limited risks charges a low premium, and a policy that protects against a great number of risks charges a high premium. The insurance value is calculated as the **cost of goods + amount of freight + insurance premium + a percentage of profit** on the sale of goods. Sometimes, to minimize the risk of losses, the buyer may request to have the goods covered for a higher percentage, which will lead to an increase in the insurance premium. In that case, the extra premium will be for the buyer's account.

The scope of possible insurance coverage varies. Usually, it is classified into two types: basic risks and additional risks.

● Basic risks

There are three types of the basic insurance coverage in marine insurance provided by PICC:

a. Free from Particular Average	F. P. A.	平安险,单独海损不赔。其责任范围包括规定的6种自然灾害和意外事故中造成的损失或产生的费用。
b. With Particular Average	W. P. A.	水渍险,又称"单独海损险",指单独海损负责赔偿。
c. All Risks		一切险,又称"综合险"。除承保平安险、水渍险全部责任外,还承保保险货物在运输过程中因各种外来原因所造成的全部和部分损失保险。

- Additional risks

Additional risks fall into two types: General Additional Risks and Special Additional Risks.

General additional risks

TPND (theft, pilferage and non-delivery)	偷窃,提货不着险
Fresh Water Rain Damage	淡水雨淋险
Risk of Shortage	短量险
Risk of Intermixture and Contamination	混杂玷污险
Risk of Leakage	渗漏险
Risk of Clash and Breakage	碰损破碎险
Risk of Odor	串味险
Damage Caused by Heating and Sweating	受热受潮险
Hook Damage	钩损险
Risk of Rust	生锈险
Loss for Damage Caused by Breakage of Packing	包装破裂险

Special additional risks

War Risk	战争险
Strikes, Riots & Civil Commotions(S. R. C. C.)	罢工暴动民变险
Failure to Delivery Risk	交货不到险

(2) Decide who will secure the insurance and decide who pays. How much control do you want with your shipment? Your terms of sale usually determine this. The seller's liability ends at the point in which the title to the goods(物权)changes from the seller to the buyer.

(3) Leave a paper trail. No matter who arranges and pays for the insurance, there are specific documents you must be prepared to present in the event of a claim. When you file a claim, you must present the following.

- A *letter of claim* along with a copy of the *bill of lading* covering the shipment.
- A copy of an *insurance certificate* prepared by your transport company or, if you purchased insurance through an independent carrier, by you.
- A *survey report* issued by a claim agent, plus an invoice showing the amount of damage or loss.

2. Writing structure

(1) Requesting or confirming insurance arrangement

The involved parties might exchange ideas on issues about coverage, premium, excessive insurance, payment of extra expenses, insurance policy etc. In most cases, insurance terms are included in the contract when a transaction is concluded on a certain basis. It is common to notify the other party to get the goods insured before delivery.

When writing such emails, we usually include the following parts.

- Confirm the order number of the goods to be insured.

Module 8　Packing, Shipment and Insurance
模块 8　包装、装运和保险

- Explain clearly how the insurance will be arranged.
- Show gratitude for understanding and cooperation.
- Express hope for a prompt reply.

(2) Dealing with a request concerning insurance arrangement

When dealing with a request concerning insurance coverage from our customers, we usually write in the following structure.

- Confirm receipt of the request.
- Reply whether such a request can be met or not; if yes, notify the sender of what has been done upon the request; if not, give a reason.
- Express willingness for further cooperation.

Section 2　Samples

Sample 1　inquire about insurance

Subject: Insurance for Electronic Toys[1]

Dear Ms. Chen,

Thanks for your email quoting us electronic toys on a CIF basis.[2] As we are in an open agreement with our underwriter, we prefer you send us a quotation on a CFR basis.[3]

However, we would be interested to know what benefits we are likely to get if our consignments are covered at your end.

Hope to have your reply soon.

Best regards,
Fred Picker

Comments

1. 没有签订合同之前,电子邮件的主题可直接写明"Insurance for ×××(产品名称)",交易达成后用电子邮件沟通时,主题中应标明订单号,以方便对方确认。
2. 以 CIF 条款进行的交易,由卖方负责投保。
3. 以 CFR 条款进行的交易,通常由买家负责投保。

Core Vocabulary

basis	*n.* 方式、准则
on basis	以……的方式/准则做某事
underwriter	*n.* 承保人,保险商
consignment	*n.* 装运的货物,运送物

Sample 2　provide insurance information (reply to Sample 1)

Subject: Re: Insurance for Electronic Toys

Dear Mr. Picker,

In reply to your email asking us to quote on a CFR basis, attached is our CFR quotation for the toys. We're sure you will find our prices workable.

We usually insured the goods sold on a CIF basis with our underwriter, the People's Insurance Company of China (PICC), for 110% of the total invoice value against All Risks. If a higher percentage of broader coverage is required, the extra premium will be for the buyer's account.

PICC is one of the leading insurers in the world and is known for settling claims promptly and equitably. The rates they quote are also quite competitive. Please check the attachment for information about their coverage and rates.

Looking forward to receiving your order soon.

Best regards,
Alice Chen

Comments

依据惯例，以发票金额的110%进行投保。如果超出这个范围，额外的费用由提出此要求的一方负担。

Core Vocabulary

for one's account	（费用）由……来负担
settle claims	（保险公司）赔付
workable	adj. 可行的
equitably	adv. 公平合理地

Sample 3　ask for insurance arrangement

Subject: Insurance for Your Order No. 616

Dear Henry,

We would like to refer you to your Order No. 616 for 1 200 dozen delivery drones which you placed on CFR[1] basis with us.

We would like to inform you that the goods are now ready for delivery and we hope that you will arrange to insure the goods against All Risks at invoice value plus 10% as soon as possible. Or, if you would like us to insure the goods on your behalf in our area,[1] please let us know without any delay.

We are looking forward to your favorable reply.

Best regards,
Rocky

Comments

1. 以CFR条款进行的交易,通常由买家负责投保。根据实际情况,买方也可以委托卖方代为办理保险。

Core Vocabulary

delivery drone	送货无人机
invoice value	发票金额

Sample 4　confirm extra insurance coverage

Subject: Re: About Excessive Insurance[1]

Dear Mr. Picker,

We have received your email of September 15th, requiring us to provide insurance for your order for an amount of 30% above the invoice value. In reply, we have arranged insurance on 500 pieces of vacuum cleaners for 130% of the invoice value against All Risks with the PICC.

The relevant insurance policy is now being prepared accordingly and will be forwarded to you very soon together with our debit note for the premium. Upon receipt of our debit note, we hope the extra premium shall be refunded to our account without any delay. Please take note of the above information.

Best regards,
Alisa

Comments

1. 客户之前发邮件要求提高参保金额,这是对客户要求的回复。

Core Vocabulary

excessive	*adj.* 超出的,过度的
policy	*n.* 保险单,政策

forward	v. 发送,寄出,提出
debit note	欠条
refund	v. 退款,偿付
take note(of sth)	注意到,将……铭记在心

Sample 5　confirm insurance arrangement

Subject：Re：Arrange Insurance
Dear Mr. Picker, We are pleased to receive your email asking us to arrange insurance on the shipment for your account. We are pleased to confirm having insured the above shipment with the People's Insurance Co. of China against All Risks for USD 3 400. The insurance policy and our debit note for the premium will be sent to you in a few days.[1] Best wishes, Alisa

Comments

1. 客户之前发邮件要求卖方代为办理保险,这里确认已代为办理。

Section 3　Core Phrases and Sentence Patterns

Phrases for talking about insurance arrangement

(1) 表示"办理保险":secure/arrange/cover/effect insurance。

(2) Insurance/insure 后接介词的用法。

- 表示所保的货物,后接 on,如:insurance on the 100 tons of wool。
- 表示投保的险别,后接 against,如:insurance against All Risks。
- 表示保额,后接 for,如:insurance for 110% of the invoice value。
- 表示保险费或保险费率,后接 at,如:insurance at the rate of 5%。
- 表示向哪家保险公司投保,后接 with,如:insurance with the PICC。
- The shipment is to be covered against all risks by the seller for 110% of the invoice value. 此批货物应由卖方按发票金额的110%投保。
- We have covered the goods with the People's Insurance Company of China against All Risks. 我们已与中国人民保险公司将货物投保一切险。
- We have arranged insurance on the 500 pieces of woolen blankets for 130% of the invoice value against All Risks with the PICC. 我们已与中国人民保险公司将500件毛毯按发票金额的130%投保一切险。

(3) 表示"代表某人投保":on sb's behalf/on behalf of sb.。

If you would like us to insure the goods on your behalf in our area, please let us know. 若想要我方代替你方为货物投保,请告知。

(4) 表示"保险费记在……的账上,由……来负担":for one's account。

We are pleased to arrange insurance on the captioned shipment for your account. 我方非常高兴为指定货物投保,费用由你方承担。

Tips

国际贸易中的投保事宜

国际贸易中的保险问题主要包含以下三个方面。

1. 谁来投保

(1) 根据合同的规定,国际贸易中常见的三种贸易术语对买卖双方都设定了各自的责任,如 FOB 和 CFR 情况下,购买保险是买方的责任;CIF 情况下,购买保险是卖方的责任。

(2) 对于贸易合同,凡是按 CIF 价格成交的出口合同,卖方在装船前,须及时到保险公司办理投保手续,填制投保单。

2. 投保什么险

(1) 如果合同上没有明确规定,则负责购买保险的一方只要按最基本的原则购买保险即可,如 CIF 可以投保平安险。

(2) 但是如果买方提出额外要求,如要求投保一切险以及附加险,则卖方应照办(即在合同上规定),但额外的保费则由买方负责(这是国际贸易的惯例,谁提出谁付钱)。

3. 投保金额

(1) 保险公司一般按 CIF 价格加成 10% 计算(即发票金额的 110%)。加成 10% 是作为国外买方的费用和预期的利润。

(2) 出口货物保险金额和保险费可按以下公式计算:保险金额=CIF 价格×110%(投保加成);保险费=CIF 价格×110%×保险费率。

在撰写有关投保事宜的函电时,应提及上一次书信往来的内容或告知对方订单或合同编号,以方便对方快速确认;要在函件中明确保险范围、保额等具体事项。函件措辞必须准确而严谨,对保险的相关要素表达必须精确,避免产生不必要的纠纷,影响交易的完成和今后进一步的合作。

Communication Laboratory

I. Translate the following phrases.

运输包装	指示标志	包装指示

续表

防水材料	包装要求	直达班轮
运费预付	海运提单	装运通知
分批装运	易碎产品	装箱单

II. Find the items equivalent to those given in Chinese below.

1. to cover insurance
2. insurance policy
3. insurance premium
4. insurance coverage
5. invoice value
6. All Risks
7. War Risk
8. Hook Damage Risk
9. for buyer's account
10. insurer
11. F. P. A. (Free from Particular Average)
12. extra premium
13. W. P. A. (With Particular Average)
14. insurance amount/value
15. premium rate
16. Shortage Risk

A( ) 保险费
B( ) 发票金额
C( ) 战争险
D( ) 承保人
E( ) 保险范围
F( ) 钩损险
G( ) 由买方支付
H( ) 额外保险费
I( ) 一切险
J( ) 保险金额
K( ) 水渍险
L( ) 保险单
M( ) 投保
N( ) 短量险
O( ) 保险费率
R( ) 平安险

III. Translate the following sentences into English.

1. 货物以2公斤装一个塑料袋,10个塑料袋装一个木箱。

2. 我们希望1个尼龙袋装1件货物,20件装成1纸箱,纸箱内衬防水材料。

Module 8 Packing, Shipment and Insurance
模块 8 包装、装运和保险

3. 请在外包装上标明"小心装卸"或"易碎品"字样。

4. 我们希望货物将会完好无损地到达贵处并能完全满足贵方的要求。

5. 我们可以满足贵方使用这种特殊包装材料的要求,但额外的包装费必须由贵方承担。

6. 我们高兴地告诉贵方,568 号订单下的货物已于今天上午装船起运。

7. 我们随函附上一整套包括提单、发票、装箱单和保险单在内的运输单据副本。

8. 我们将额外投保破碎险,费用由你方负担。

9. 根据你方要求,我们将按发票金额的 110% 投保。

IV. Fill in the missing words in the blanks of the following letter.

Dear Sirs,

　　In ___1___ (回复) to your letter urging the shipment, we ___2___ (遗憾) being unable to ship the 10 containers of Chinese animal plush toys ___3___ (通过) direct steamers.

　　The direct steamers are very rare from here to your ___4___ (港口) and the shipping space has been fully ___5___ (预定) up to the end of the month after next. Therefore we would suggest that you ___6___ (允许) us to ship via Hong Kong and such arrangement will result in the ___7___ (准时) arrival of the cargo.

We hope you understand that we are not the only exporter who has difficulty in __8__ （预定）shipping space.

We look forward to __9__ （收到）your early confirmation on this __10__ （事项）.

Yours faithfully,

Li Hua

V. Write an email in English based on the Situation given.

1. 按照下列中文提示资料撰写装船通知。

（1）信用证号码：CNHL654321；开证日期：210402；

（2）发票编号：ICED052021；金额：USD 14 800.00；

（3）数量：500 个纸箱共装 2 500 套咖啡杯碟（cup and saucer）；

（4）总毛重：8MT；总体积：27CBM；

（5）承运人：TRANSWORLD；船名：Eastern Star；航次：V.013；

（6）提单编号：B/L No. COS2105460；签发日期：June 10,2021；

（7）申请人：F&T TRADING Co., LTD.；

（8）受益人：HUAYI Co., LTD.；

（9）预期到达时间：EARLY JULY；

（10）装运后 48 小时内应发出装船通知；

（11）额外投保破碎险，按发票金额的 120% 投保。

2. 客户(Indigo Co., Ltd., 联系人 Alison Fillmore)向我方公司订购了 100 台打印机（订单号 PT024），货物已于 2021 年 10 月 7 日发出，预计一周后到达。100 台打印机分 5 箱包装，每箱上均标有▲标记。我方通过 DHL 寄给客户如下装运单据：第 IV014 号发票一份，第 NYKS400158610 提单一份，第 PKD004152 号装箱单一份。请写电子邮件告知客户。

Subject:

Content:

Module 9 After-sales Follow-up

模块 9
售后跟进

Learning Goals

❖ Know about the key points of following up after completion of order.
❖ Be able to use words, expressions and sentence patterns to write after-sales follow-up letters.
❖ Be able to write effective after-sales follow-up letters in the hope of engaging and re-engaging existing customers and strengthening business relations.

Lead-in

Situation: Now you've completed a deal with a foreign client. What would you do next?
Questions:
1. How to know the products or services' acceptance in the market and clients' suggestions of the product or service?
2. How do you motivate the client to buy more from us?

Task 1

Asking for Feedback

Most business people know that keeping an existing customer is far more cost-effective than trying to rope in a new one. Existing customers are the lifeblood of every business. Businesses go out of their way to keep them coming back. Thus, it makes sense to focus efforts and funds to nurture our existing customers, to engage and re-engage customers.

After-sales follow-up is a salesperson contacting his/her customer after a successful sale to achieve a few key goals.

- Making the customer feel valued.
- Ensuring the customer's needs are met by the product or service.
- Answering any questions or concerns the customer might have.
- Understanding how the salesperson might be of further service to his/her customer.

Asking for feedback is a great starting point for understanding and meeting customer expectations.

Section 1 Guidelines

Here's what we need to do if we want to send successful customer feedback emails.
- Use an attention-grabbing email subject.
- Start with a personalized salutation so they know this isn't spamming.
- Tell them why they're getting the feedback request.
- Share how we're going to use the results to benefit them.
- Give them an idea of how long the process will take (*for something structured like a survey*).
- End with thanks and a call to action.

Common feedback questions are as follows.
- What improvements in our product/service would you like to see?
- What feature(s) are you using the most?
- What feature(s) are you not using at all?
- What new feature(s) would you like to see and how would you prioritize those?
- What's different now compared to your expectations?
- Is there anything that you don't understand or that doesn't make sense to you?

Section 2 Samples

Sample 1

Hi Mr. Phupoom,

Thank you for your purchase with us. Your order should have arrived by now and we hope everything went well. Please feel free to inform us about any delays or problems you might have faced—we want to make sure you've had a good experience. [1]

We would love to know your reviews of our products and services. Would you help in answering 6 quick questions? [2]

Thanks for your time and have a great day,
Jeff Rong

Comments

1. 感谢对方向我方购买产品,提出可提供售后跟进和服务。

2. 请对方填调查问卷(以超链接形式),此时注意问卷不要过长,既方便客户快速填写,又能获取我们想得到的反馈信息。

Core Vocabulary

inform	v. 通知,告知
review	v./n. 评论,评价

Sample 2

Dear Doraraj,

We are so thrilled you've chosen to purchase Bob's Collection football jersey from us. How do you like it so far? We are working hard to build a higher quality product for our customers by listening to buyers' comments and concerns.

We would love to learn more about your opinions. Can you please fill out this survey to give us some feedback?

LINK TO OUR FEEDBACK SURVEY

Our goal is to continue offering top-notch products at good prices, and your review could greatly help us to continue doing so.

I really appreciate you taking out the time to help us improve our offerings!

Thank you,
Lin Hua

Core Vocabulary

thrilled	adj. 非常兴奋的,极为激动的
concern	v./n. 关切,关心
appreciate	v. 感激,感谢
offering	n. 待售品,出售品
top-notch	adj. 最好的,卓越的,一流的

Sample 3

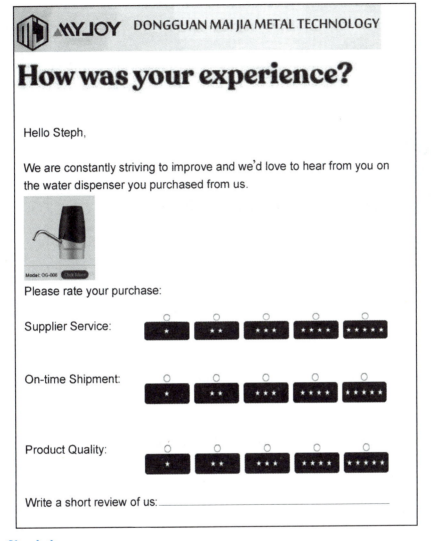

Core Vocabulary

constantly   *adv.* 始终，一直
strive   *v.* 努力，奋斗，力争

Section 3 | Core Phrases and Sentence Patterns

1. Expressing thanks for customer's purchase
- Thank you for purchasing LED lights from us.
- I notice that you've made a few orders with us. I just wanted to reach out and say huge thanks.
- We really appreciate your order of water dispensers.
- We are so thrilled you've chosen to purchase a football jersey from us.

2. Asking about sales or feedback
- Please feel free to inform us about any delays or problems you might have faced.
- We would love to know your reviews of our products and services.
- We'd appreciate it if you could give us your feedback. Your suggestions will be most helpful for us.
- Your review could greatly help us to continue improving our products.
- Your suggestions will be most helpful for us.

Task 2 Introducing Latest Products

Section 1 | Guidelines

A great product launch email is one of our best opportunities to re-engage customers and remind them of the value our product provides. Naturally, our email strategy depends on the brand, product, and relationship with customers. So while there's no formula for the perfect product launch email, here are tips to get inspired.
- Work on your email subject line.
- Use compelling product images. A picture speaks a thousand words. Use high-quality product images to make sure the potential customers can't help but buy it.

Also, asking for their opinion in our email will let them know you value what they say and help introduce them to new products without being too pushy.

In addition, when we would like to introduce an existing customer to something they haven't ordered yet, we can send samples and survey their opinion as an after-sale technique to drum up more business.

Section 2 | Samples

Sample 1 introduce new products and invite opinions

Subject: Latest Automatic Smart USB Rechargeable Water Dispenser
Dear Steve,   We are now launching a new series of water dispensers. In the past years, our water dispensers sell well in the European market. Would you like to evaluate the samples? I'm sure the new series is good for promotion.¹

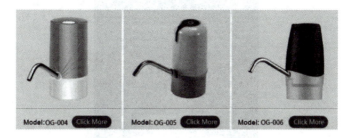

We are interested in developing some new products, especially for your market. Do you have some ideas in terms of designs, features and/or functions? We'd love to have your opinions.²

Best regards,
Jill

Comments

1. 告知对方我公司正在推出新产品,提出可寄样品供评估。
2. 邀请对方对产品的设计、特色、功能等提出建议。

Core Vocabulary

automatic	*adj.* 自动的
rechargeable	*adj.* 可再充电的
smart	*adj.* 智能的
dispenser	*adj.* (取款、售货等用的)自动取物装置

Sample 2   introduce new products

Subject: Latest Portable Juice Blender Cup

Dear James,

I'm attaching a file of the product specification of our latest portable juice blender cup. It's an improved version of the juice blender cup you purchased from us. Its battery capacity is 20% larger than the previous model.

The new model costs 10% more. We will send a sample to you upon request.

Click here for more details.

Best regards,
Wendy

Core Vocabulary

portable   *adj.* 便携式的
blender   *n.* (食物)搅拌器

Sample 3   introduce new products

Dear Dan,

I want to check with you about your last order for the tools kit set. How is the business going there? Are you making a good profit by selling our new products? Or do you have any problems?

We'd appreciate it if you could give us your feedback. Your suggestions will be most helpful for us.

Now we've developed a similar set that uses heat-treated CRV steel with stronger toughness and hardness. Please check the attachment for details.

Looking forward to hearing from you soon!

Thanks & Best Regards,
Jack

Core Vocabulary

tools kit set	工具组合套装
toughness	n. 韧性

Extended Vocabulary

CrV steel (chromium-vanadium steel)	铬钒钢，是掺有碳、锰、硅、铬和钒的合金钢。

Section 3 Core Phrases and Sentence Patterns

Introducing new product

- Recently we released a new product Meya SD 301 air conditioner.
- We are glad to introduce our newly launched sports bracelet to you.
- We've developed a similar set that is tougher and more durable. Please check the attachment for details.

Task 3 Offering Discounts

Section 1 Guidelines

The key to keeping our communications from sounding one-sided is that we're not just asking for orders all the time or sending junk offers. Sending customers a personalized coupon can be an effective marketing strategy. It works great because clients want to feel like they're important to our business and such a personal touch can work wonders for our sales.

Section 2 Samples

Sample 1 send a personalized coupon

Subject: Smart Bracelet Newly Launched

Hi Mr. Barineg,

I notice that you've made a few orders with us this month already.

I just wanted to reach out and say great thanks. We really appreciate it.[1]

If you have anything else you need to pick up before the month is out, I've created a special coupon just for you to get a further 5% off whatever you're ordering.[2]

Thanks again, I hope you enjoy the rest of the month!

Best regards,
Rocky

Comments

1. 感谢客户这个月的重复下单。
2. 给客户提供专属优惠券。

Core Vocabulary

reach out　　　　　　联系
coupon　　　　　　　n. 优惠券

Sample 2　give a special offer

To: fred_Bicket@mek.com
From: alisa_chen@weichi.com
Subject: Special Discount for the 10th Anniversary

Dear Mr. Bicket,

How are you?

We are pleased to advise you that it will be the 10th anniversary of the founding of Weichi on September 15. To express gratitude to old customers, we are going to launch a promotion from September 1 to September 20.

So, Dear Mr. Bicket, if you have new demand recently, you can order within this promotion period and you will enjoy a special discount (up to **15% off**). We hope you won't miss it.

Waiting for your reply soon.

Best regards,

Alisa

Comments

本邮件以公司 10 周年庆典作为理由，与老客户联系，提供优惠折扣，吸引老客户下单。

Core Vocabulary

anniversary	n. 周年纪念日
gratitude	n. 感谢（的心情），感激
promotion	n. 推销，促销

Section 3　Core Phrases and Sentence Patterns

Offer a special discount

- I've created a special coupon just for you to get a further 5% off.
- We do not often offer special discounts, so we are very happy to announce that we will be having a huge discount sale from November 11 to 21.
- For any orders for the following items, we are offering a special discount of 10%.
- As a gesture of goodwill, we're creating a special discount of 12% on your account.

Tips

如何做好外贸业务的售后跟进

在产品同质化竞争愈演愈烈的今天，服务在外贸活动中至关重要。我们的售后邮件，除了询问客户的反馈意见，介绍新品或促销信息等，还可以包含如下内容。

1. 产品的安装说明、示意图或者视频

对于需要自行安装的产品，可能会有附带的使用说明书，但如果有图册或者示意图，甚至安装视频，附在产品包装内，或在售后邮件发给客户供参考，会更加方便客户，让客户感受到周到细致的服务。

2. 产品使用和保养的小窍门、小技巧

在产品交货后，贴心地发送产品使用和保养的小窍门或者注意事项，例如，使用中需要注意哪些事项便可以延长产品的使用年限，或者怎样使用产品能够发挥其最好效果，或者当产品需要 A 产品做搭配时，如果没有 A，产品 B 也可以暂时代替 A 等小窍门。这些贴心的提示，对产品销售和推广都有好处，可以让客户对我们的专业性和信任度有所提升。

3. 产品常见问题和解决

产品在使用和销售过程中常遇到哪些问题，通常有什么处理或者解决办法，都可以总结为一个文档发给客户。

4. 产品卖点和优势

售后服务应该包括提供产品详细卖点和参数信息文档,这一方面为客户省去了大量研究产品、编辑销售推广内容的时间,另一方面可以统一产品宣传内容,保持权威性和一致性,给终端客户一个专业的形象。

认真写好售后跟进邮件,能帮我们获得不少客户。

Communication Laboratory

I. Fill in each of the following blanks with a proper word/words given in the box. Change the form where necessary.

coupon	launch	anniversary	version
rate	survey		

1. Our company has recently _____ a low-cost "network computer" to the market.
2. The company is celebrating its twentieth _____ this year.
3. Please _____ your purchase in terms of quality, shipment, etc.
4. Can you please fill out this _____ to give us some feedback?
5. It's an improved _____ of the LED TV you purchased from us.
6. I've created a special _____ just for you to get a further 10% discount.

II. Please write up sentences based on the following situations.

1. 我方想告诉客户,最近推出了一款冰箱,特点是节能和噪音小。

   _____

2. 我方想通知客户,今年是我们公司成立15周年,我们推出了老客户在6月1日至15日下订单享受最高8.8折优惠活动。

   _____

3. 我方希望收集客户的意见和建议时,如何跟客户说?

   _____

4. 有一个客户去年没有下订单,我方想跟进客户,了解他没有下单的原因,以便改善产品和服务,可以怎样写给客户?

   _____

5. 前两个月卖了一款产品给客户,现在我方想了解这款产品在客户的市场卖得好不好,可以怎样问客户?

_____
_____

III. Write an email in English based on the situation given.

我方的公司名为 GELA Co., Ltd., 是各种空调的生产商和出口商, 斯里兰卡客商 Amalig 公司(email: aml@gil.com, 联系人: Mr. Bricket)前几年都下订单, 但是去年没有下订单。借今年本公司 5 周年年庆与他联系, 了解他去年没有下订单的原因, 请他对本公司的产品和服务提意见, 并且特别强调, 今年公司 5 周年年庆, 优惠老客户, 如果他能在 7 月下订单, 可以享受 9 折优惠。

Subject: _____

Content:
_____
_____
_____
_____
_____
_____
_____
_____
_____
_____
_____
_____
_____

IV. Practical Writing.

Visit alibaba.com and find out a company you're interested in. Suppose you are a salesperson in this company and your company has recently launched a new product. Then write an email to one of your old customers to promote the new product.

Subject: _____

Content:
_____
_____
_____
_____
_____

Module  Complaints and Claims

模块 10

投诉与索赔

Learning Goals

◆ Know about key points to write a complaint or a claim.
◆ Be able to use words, expressions and sentence patterns to write complaints or claims.
◆ Know about how to lodge complaints or claims in the business situation.

Lead-in

Situations:

1. One of your clients complains to you that the goods delivered are short in weight.

2. One of your clients makes a claim against your company, complaining that the goods delivered are not in conformity with the sample. According to the client, he suffers a great loss and thus demands compensation from your company.

Question:

1. How would you reply to the complaint?

2. How would you reply to the claim?

Writing and Replying to Complaints

What might be the causes for complaints in international trade?

When a seller fails to deliver his goods, or a buyer fails to fulfill his payment obligation, or the two parties have different understandings, or one of the parties intentionally creates disputes, complaints may arise.

Section 1　Guidelines

1. Making complaints

A good complaint letter should be concise, authoritative, factual, constructive and friendly. Here are some tips.

(1) Provide a time limit. A time limit will prompt the recipient to act immediately.

(2) Attach supporting documents. These could be images, receipts, and other documents that serve as concrete evidence of your claims.

When making complaints, your letter should:

(1) mention the date of the order, the date of delivery and the goods you complained about.

(2) regret the need to complain.

(3) state your reasons for being dissatisfied or asking for an explanation.

(4) refer to the inconvenience caused.

(5) suggest how to solve the matter.

2. Replying to complaints

After receiving a complaint, how we address it can have a tremendous influence on customer retention. By addressing customer's specific issues successfully, we can turn a negative situation into a positive experience and continue to develop long-term relationships. Below are some tips on writing in response to complaints.

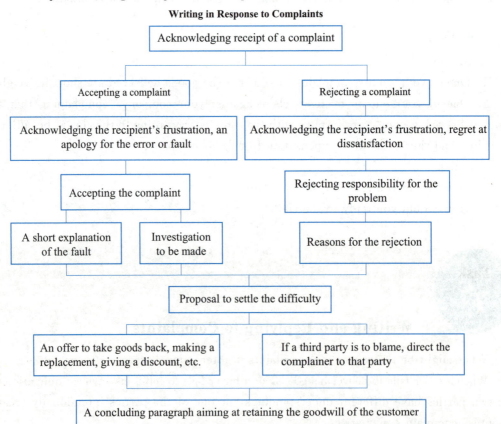

Writing in Response to Complaints

Module 10 Complaints and Claims
模块 10 投诉与索赔

Section 2 Samples

Sample 1 make a complaint

Subject: Shortfall of Order No. 76819L [1]

Dear Ms. Yang,

I am writing to inform you that the goods we ordered from your company have not been supplied correctly. [2]

On January 15, 2021, we placed an order with your firm for 11 000 mini fans. The consignment arrived yesterday but contained only 1 100 mini fans. [3]

This error put us in a difficult position, as we had to make some emergency purchases to fulfill our commitments to all our customers. This caused us considerable inconvenience. [4]

I am writing to ask you to make up the shortfall immediately and ensure that such errors do not happen again. Otherwise, we may have to look elsewhere for our supplies. [5]

I look forward to hearing from you in return.

Yours sincerely,
Valery Bakhtov
Purchasing Officer

Comments
1. 电子邮件的主题要能简要概括投诉事项。
2. 表明写信目的。
3. 说明情况。
4. 说明对方的错误给己方造成的不良影响。
5. 表明希望对方采取的补救行动。

Sample 2 accept a complaint (reply to Sample 1)

Subject: Re: Order No. 76819L [1]

Dear Mr. Bakhtov,

Please accept our apologies for the error made by our company in filling your order No. 76819L. [2]

You ordered 11 000 mini fans, but our dispatch office sent 1 100. This was due to a typing error.³

The balance of 9 900 fans was dispatched by SF express(click here to track the package) to you this morning and will arrive by Thursday, January 28, 2021.⁴

We highly value your business and would like to offer you an 8% discount on your next order with us.⁵

We look forward to receiving your further orders and assure you that they will be filled correctly.⁶

Yours sincerely,
Alisa Yang
Sales Manager

Comments

1. 此处改掉了对方的电子邮件主题,只保留中性意义的订单号,避免对方再次感受"shortfall"一词带来的消极情绪。
2. 调查后,如发现确实是我方失误,第一时间真诚道歉。
3. 解释原因。
4. 表明整改措施,以期获得对方信任,维持合作关系。
5. 给予适当的补偿,例如下次下单,可获8%折扣。
6. 再次承诺整改,期待继续合作。

Core Vocabulary

fill one's order	交付订货
dispatch	v./n. 发送
express	n. 快递服务

Sample 3　reject a complaint（reply to Sample 1）

Subject: Re: Order No. 76819L
Attachment: Order Form No. 76819L

Dear Mr. Bakhtov,

Thank you for your email regarding your order No. 76819L. We understand that this is a difficult situation for you.¹

We have investigated the situation and found that you ordered 1 100 mini fans. Please see the attached order form.² Our dispatch office, therefore, sent 1 100.

If you need the remaining goods urgently, the balance of 9 900 fans can be dispatched today by express courier to you and would arrive by Thursday, January 28, 2021.³

Please tell me if you would like to order these fans.

We look forward to receiving your further orders.

Yours sincerely,
Alisa Yang
Sales Manager

Comments
1. 感谢对方的邮件，对对方的处境表示理解。
2. 说明我方的调查结果，表明并非我方失误，并附上证据。
3. 提出解决方案。

Core Vocabulary

| investigate | v. 调查 |
| express courier | 快递公司 |

Sample 4 make a complaint

Subject: Incomplete Shipment of Order DT-20314

Dear Ms. Chen,

The shipment we received with order number DT-20314 was incomplete. The following parts were missing.

panel #1256, 10pcs

cable #147, 20pcs¹

We would appreciate it if you would rush the missing parts to us immediately.² Thank you for your prompt attention to this matter.

Sincerely,
Riichi Tanaka

Comments

1. 若需要投诉的事项或涉及的物品比较多,可用清楚明了的方式一一列出。
2. 提出希望对方采取的补救行动。

Core Vocabulary

panel   n. 仪表板,面板
cable   n. 电缆,缆绳

Sample 5   accept a complaint（reply to Sample 4）

Subject：Re：Incomplete Shipment of Order DT-20314

Dear Mr. Tanaka,

Thank you for your email informing us of the incomplete shipment of Order DT-20314. We are extremely sorry to learn that some parts are missing from the shipment.[1]

The missing parts were sent this morning by DHL.[2] You may click here to track delivery→.

We greatly regret the inconvenience. To prevent re-occurrences, we have set up a verification procedure. We assure you that this will not happen again.[3]

Yours sincerely,
Alisa Chen

Comments

1. 表明已收到对方的投诉,并表达歉意。
2. 说明已经采取的补救措施。
3. 再次表达歉意,并承诺已整改,不会发生类似错误,以求重获客户的信任。

Core Vocabulary

inconvenience   n. 不便,麻烦
occurrence   n. 发生
verification   n. 核实,查证
procedure   n. 程序,步骤,工序

Sample 6   accept a complaint

Subject：Re：Disqualified Anti-virus Masks

Dear Fred,

I am sorry to know that the masks of Order No. 508 delivered to you don't match the samples. After investigation, we found the quality of the goods is indeed not in conformity with the samples. This occurs because one warehouse staff mixed up your order with another one.

We will arrange replacements right away. Please send the disqualified masks back at our expense.

We apologize for the inconvenience caused and assure you that we have instituted a double-checking system for order dispatch so that this mistake will not happen again in future deliveries.

Best regards,

Alisa

Core Vocabulary

in conformity with	和……一致
warehouse	n. 仓库
at one's expense	费用由某人承担
institute	v. 建立,制定
double-checking system	双重检验体系

Section 3 Core Phrases and Sentence Patterns

1. Making complaints

- I would like to make/lodge/lay/file a complaint with you about the shortfall of the goods we received.
- I am writing to inform you of my dissatisfaction with the goods you supplied to us.
- Upon examination, we found the goods are not up to the standard of the sample.
- The goods sent are inferior compared to the original sample.
- I am writing to ask you to make up the shortfall immediately and ensure that such errors do not happen again.
- Otherwise, we may have to look elsewhere for our supplies.

2. Accepting complaints

- Thank you for your letter of… regarding/concerning/in connection with…
- I refer to your letter of… about / relating to…
- We agree that the usual high standards of our products/services were not met in this instance.
- I will contact you tomorrow when I have more information about the problem.

- I will let you know/get in touch with you after we take care of it.
- Let me find out what happened to your order/item and I will get back to you shortly/later today.
- To prevent re-occurrences we have set up a verification procedure.
- The product team is making it their priority to ensure this problem does not happen again.
- As a gesture of our regret, we are prepared to…/we are willing to…/we would like to…
- We have dispatched the new items by express courier. They should arrive by Thursday, 21 December, 2021.
- We propose to have the goods inspected first. If the inspection confirms the accuracy of your estimate, compensation will be allowed at once.
- To show our goodwill, we would like to offer you a 5% discount on your next order with us.
- I have an update for you regarding your order. We have your replacement unit ready to be shipped out to you this morning. You should be receiving it in 2-3 days.
- Right now, we're working on your item. We just have a few more tests to run. Once everything's okay, we'll be in touch again.
- We should be able to get your problem resolved (soon/in a couple of days/within this week).

3. Rejecting complaints
- While we can understand your frustration, …
- We understand how disappointing it can be when your expectations are not met.
- I regret to say that I don't think the responsibility should rest with us.
- Although we have sent you the correct item, if you are dissatisfied with it, we are happy to exchange it.
- I regret to inform you that…
- I am afraid that…
- Unfortunately, I must point out that…

Writing and Replying to Claims

In international business, complaints or claims do not happen in every transaction but often occur. In the course of executing a contract, if one party fails to perform the contract and brings economic loss to another party, the latter may lodge a claim for compensation according to the contract stipulations.

Causes of loss vary with different ranges of responsibility, and different parties will be liable for the claim lodged. If the seller breaches the contract(e. g. non-delivery or delay of delivery, short weight or shortage of quantity, inferior quality, improper packing, etc.), which incurs a loss, the seller will shoulder the responsibility and the buyer should lodge a claim against him or her according to the contract regulations. If the buyer breaches the contract (e. g. non-payment or delay of payment, etc.), he or she will be responsible for the loss sustained and the seller should claim with him or her on an actual case. If the loss takes place during transit, it is within the responsibility of the insurance company or the shipping company and the party that suffered loss should file a claim.

Section 1　Guidelines

1. Making claims

A good claiming letter should also be concise, authoritative and factual. It usually includes the following main points.

(1) Giving facts about the loss (quoting the file number, the date of delivery, the goods concerned, etc.) and reasons why the recipient should be responsible.

(2) Analyzing any possible impacts.

(3) Hoping for an early solution to the problem.

2. Responding to claims

When replying to claims, follow the rules below.

(1) Confirming receipt of claims.

(2) Showing regret for what has happened and sincere wish for resolving the problem.

(3) Promising to look into the matter carefully.

(4) When accepting the claim, put forward the proposals for settling the problem; when rejecting the claim, make specific and justified explanation.

(5) Showing enthusiasm to continue the business relations with the clients and wishing for further cooperation.

Note: All replies should be based on a thorough investigation of the whole matter. Never give an answer before your settlement got approved by your boss.

Section 2　Samples

Sample 1　make a claim

Subject: Torn Cartons!! (Order No. ST256)

Dear Mr. Feng,

We received this afternoon the 30 cartons of Woolen Carpet under our Order No. ST256. The shipping agent noticed that Carton No. 28 was torn. We immediately had the carton opened and the contents examined by a local surveyor in the presence of the shipping agent. Clearly, the carton was broken and the carpets were in the open. This is obviously the result of improper packing.¹

Though the carpets can be used, we have to sell them at a price much lower than usual.² So we would like either replacement of the items or a 20% reduction in price³.

Attached are the surveyor's report and the shipping agents' statement.⁴

Please let us know your decision as soon as possible.

Kind regards,
Yosuf Aihamed

Comments
1. 简要陈述事实,分析原因。
2. 说明造成的后果。
3. 提出赔偿方案。
4. 附上证明材料。

Core Vocabulary

shipping agent	船运代理
surveyor	n. 检测员
in the presence of	在……在场的情况下
statement	n. 声明;陈述

Sample 2   respond to a claim (reply to Sample 1)

Subject: Packing of Carton 28 (Order No. ST256)

Dear Mr. Aihamed,

We regret to know that Carton No. 28 was torn and we are terribly sorry for this incident. We have checked with our warehouse and discovered the carton was not packed as specified in the contract. This was due to the negligence of our warehouse staff.¹

To compensate for this negative experience, we agree to give you a 20% discount on the invoice value for carpets in Carton 28.² We have set up a verification procedure in packing and assure you that this will not happen again.³

Yours faithfully,
Fred Feng
Sales Manager

Module 10 Complaints and Claims
模块 10 投诉与索赔

Comments

1. 真诚道歉，并说明造成错误出现的原因。
2. 同意对方提出的赔偿方案。
3. 表示已经整改，确保不会发生类似错误，以求重获客户的信任。

Core Vocabulary

negligence   *n.* 疏忽，失误

Sample 3   make a claim

Subject: Claim for Poor Quality Mini Fans

Dear Frank,

Up to now, we have received several claims from our customers on the mini fans under Contract No. GZ109. After inspection, we found that the arrival is not in exact conformity with the samples you sent us before signing the contract. This is unacceptable, and we have to recall all items RIGHT NOW and compensate our customers.

You are requested to give us a full refund and bear all charges of this recall. Attached is a list of recall charges. You are requested to remit the amount to our bank account, details of which are attached with this email.

We are looking forward to your early settlement.

Best regards,
Alisa

Core Vocabulary

inspection	*n.* 检验
recall	*v.* 召回（残损货品等）
refund	*v./n.* 退款，返还金额
remit	*v.* 汇款

Sample 4   respond to a claim (reply to Sample 3)

Subject: Compensation for Mini Fans

Dear Alisa,

We are sorry that all items should be recalled. However, we sent you the final samples before mass production and they were confirmed by your engineering team. It is thus unfair that we should bear all responsibility for the problem.

To fix the situation, we suggest that we ship the new model of mini fans as replacements and give you USD 4 000 as compensation.

Please let me know what do you think about it.

Best regards,
Frank

Sample 5   respond to a claim

Subject: Re: Logo Printing on Sports Jerseys

Dear Mr. Carlson,

We have received your email, in which you pointed out the problem with logo printing in our sports jerseys.

We sincerely apologize for this unpleasant event. We will ship sports jerseys with correct logos immediately and they would arrive by January 27, 2021.

We have remitted USD 1 123.80 as a settlement of your claim. Please kindly inform us upon receiving them.

Regarding the jerseys with the wrong logos, our forwarder will call you later to collect them from your warehouse.

We apologize for the trouble and assure you that all possible steps will be taken by ourselves. Then we can prevent this from happening again in the future.

Kind regards,
Xu Yulin(Miss)
Sales Manager

Core Vocabulary

forwarder　　　　　　　　　　n. 代运人，货运公司

Section 3　Core Phrases and Sentence Patterns

1. Making claims

- We regret to inform you that we must lodge/file/make/place a claim against you about the quality.
- We were sorry to find fifteen cases badly damaged. None of the juice is suitable for consumption.
- We estimate that about 10% of the goods are damaged. So we would like either replacement of the items or a 10% reduction in price.
- We, therefore, suggest you give us a 30% discount on the invoice value or we will ask you for replacements.
- We can keep this delivery and try to find another buyer for it. But of course, we'd need a price adjustment, say a 25% reduction on the lot.
- We'd like you to replace all 15 sets as soon as possible. Our customer is waiting for the complete order.

2. Responding to claims

- In the spirit of goodwill and friendship, we agree to accept all your claims.
- We regret to say that we are not in a position to entertain your claim.
- I'm afraid there's been a slip-up in our Shipping Department. It's certainly our fault.
- The goods were in good order when they were shipped on board. The bill of lading signed by the captain of the ship is proof of that.
- Unfortunately, because you accepted the samples we had sent you, we won't replace the shipment.
- The goods left here in perfect condition. Was the damage caused by rough handling?
- In view of the long business relations between us, we wish to meet you halfway to settle the claim.
- This is the maximum concession(让步) we can make. Should you not agree to our proposal, we would like to settle it by arbitration(仲裁).

Tips

如何处理对外贸易中的投诉与索偿？

(1) 收到客户投诉邮件，我们要立即回复，不要拖延。即使在调研，也应先做出回复。

- I will contact you tomorrow when I have more information about the problem.
- Let me find out what happened to your order/item and I will get back to you shortly/later today/as soon as I can.

否则，若客户感到被忽视，会更加生气。

(2) 在回信时,首先表示对他的情况及心情完全理解。

- I fully understand how you must feel about having waited two weeks for the replacement part.
- We understand how disappointing it can be when your expectations are not met.
- I'm sorry to hear you are having these problems.

(3) 如果是我方的错,要立即道歉。

(4) 如果需要进一步调查情况,可跟客户说:"我们已经汇报老板,马上找相关部分的人开会,进行调查。能否提供进一步的细节,比如拍个照片,有多少货物有问题?"

(5) 如果事情已经调查清楚,要解释这个事情为何会发生,问题出在什么地方,已经采取了什么措施,并保证下次不会发生。

(6) 如果客户有责任,要委婉地指出来。

如是由于客户自己的设计缺陷导致的问题,不要说:"It is because your design is not feasible."可以说:"Our chief engineers told me that the design is a major cause of this problem. We may need to optimize the design together for the future production."展现通力合作解决问题的态度。(注意,这里用 we,而不是 I,用 we 表示代表公司的态度和整个公司通力合作的意愿。)

(7) 把客户的注意力引导到解决问题上来。

我们可引导客户,让客户感受到我们在积极努力解决问题,让客户的注意力不过多放在损失应该由谁来承担这个问题上。

It is really out of our expectations. We must find out a solution to sort it out. Do you have any ideas?

(8) 在安抚客户的同时,争取利益。例如,可以向客户许诺下个订单予以补偿。

(9) 若问题不是一下子就能解决的,要及时告知客户进展。

- I have an update for you regarding your order. We have your replacement unit ready to be shipped out to you this morning. You should be receiving it in 2－3 days.
- Right now, we're working on your item. We just have a few more tests to run. Once everything's okay, we'll be in touch again.
- We should be able to get your problem resolved (soon/in a couple of days/within this week).

总之,解决外贸中的纠纷,回应客户的投诉要掌握技巧或方法,要有建设性的态度,力求解决问题。

Communication Laboratory

I. Fill in the missing propositions or infinitives.

1. We are lodging a claim _____ the shipment _____ S/S "Far East" _____

short delivery.（我们对通过"远东号"货轮运输的货物提出短量索赔。）

2. After inspection at the port of destination, the quality of the goods shipped _____ S/S "Far East" _____ Order No. 1234 was found not _____ conformity _____ the contract stipulations.（在目的港检验后发现，1234号订单项下、经"远东"货轮运送的货物质量不符合合同规定。）

3. We regret _____ hear that several bags of the last shipment were broken _____ transit.（很遗憾，我们了解到上一批货中的几袋货物在运输过程中破损了。）

4. We are sorry to hear that the goods you received are not _____ the quality expected.（很遗憾听说您收到的货物没有达到预期的质量。）

5. The goods left here _____ perfect condition. Was it caused by rough handling?（货物离开这里的时候是完好无损的。破损是因为粗暴处理造成的吗？）

II. Fill in the missing words.

1. I would like to _____ a complaint with you about the shortfall of the goods we received.（提出投诉）

2. Thank you for your email of January 19, 2021 _____ the shortfall of Order No. 214.（关于）

3. Let me find out what happened to your order/item and I will _____ .（回复你）

4. We _____ you that this will not happen again.（保证）

5. As a gesture of our regret, we are prepared to give you a _____ .（替换）

III. Translate the following Sentences into English.

1. 从贵方9月20日的电子邮件中获知我方发错了折叠椅（fold chair），对此我方深感抱歉。

_____

2. 我们对延迟发货深表歉意，希望贵方谅解，延期的起因是我方无法控制的。

_____

3. 显然，货物是在运输途中受损，因此，抱歉很难接受贵方的索赔。

_____

4. 请代表我方向船主提出索赔，他们对这一损失负有责任。

_____

5. 我们确信，我们正在发送的用以替换的玩具将令人满意。

_____

6. 请退回破损的货品,退回费用由我方承担。
_____
_____

7. 今天汇出 2 800 美元,以支付贵方 600 公斤短重(short weight)索赔。
_____
_____

Ⅳ. Find out mistakes in the following email responding to a complaint.（The mistakes can be grammatical mistakes, punctuation mistakes or content mistakes. Be sure to find out the contents that do not conform with the guidelines for writing a response to a complaint/claim letter.）

Subject：Your Complaint
Dear Sirs I would like to apologise for the error made by our company in supplying your order number 9857/E dated 18 December 2020. You ordered 100 size-36 dresses(model no. 134) and our dispatch office sent only 10. This was due to an invoicing mistake. You also informed us that the colour of the dresses that you did receive was not consistent. You said that the colours of different dresses were slightly different shades of red, some being more of an orange colour. You also said that one of the dresses had two different shades, with the arms being lighter than the skirt. We have told our clerk to be more careful with invoicing. We have also complained to the factory about the colours. We have dispatched 100 new garments by express courier. They should arrive by Friday, 22 January 2021. To show our goodwill, we would like to offer you a 20% discount on your next order with us. We look forward to receiving your further orders and assure you that they will be filled promptly.

Yours sincerely,
Alice Chen
The Distributions Manager

V. Write an email in English based on the situation given.

Dear Sirs,

We are writing to inform you that the electronic toys covered by our order No. 525 arrived in such an unsatisfactory condition that we have to lodge a claim against you. It was found upon examination that 5% of them are broken and some are badly scratched, obviously due to the improper packing. Therefore, we cannot sell at the normal price and suggest that you make us an allowance of 20% on the invoiced cost. If you cannot accept this proposal, I'm afraid we have to return them for replacement.

Attached are some photos showing the damages to the toys.

Sincerely yours,
John Olender
Your reply to the above claim.

Subject:

Content:

Module 11 Miscellaneous Correspondence

Learning Goals

❖ Learn about basic words, expressions, sentences useful for writing auto-replies, notifications and holiday regards to business partners.

❖ Know about how to write the contents of auto-replies, notifications and holiday regards properly in actual business situations.

Lead-in

Situation:

1. The National Day holiday is coming. You decide to set an automatic reply to emails sent to you during this period. How would you write this auto-reply?

2. Your company decides to raise the prices of certain products. You would write an email to inform your clients of this decision. How would you write this email?

3. One of your clients has been promoted to Vice President. You decide to write an email to congratulate him. How would you write this email?

Setting Email Auto Replies

Introduction

Auto replies are useful for a variety of situations: when people reach out to you during your holidays, such as the National Day holiday, the Spring Festival, annual leave, sick leave, etc., or when you are out of the office for a business trip, for customer inquiries, for a quick confirmation of the receipt of orders, or for people who are simply swamped with emails. To some extent, such auto-replies can improve the efficiency of communications and reduce the workload of replies.

Section 1　Guidelines

1. Compass

The following is the auto-reply function offered by **QQ** mail.

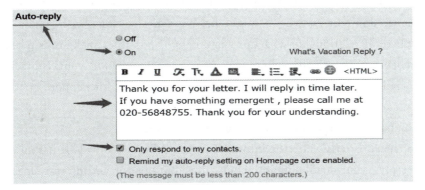

If we use email systems such as Microsoft Outlook, we can use the email system to auto-reply messages with a specific template（模板）based on some rules. Templates can contain scripting（脚本）elements to build replies that use information from the incoming message.

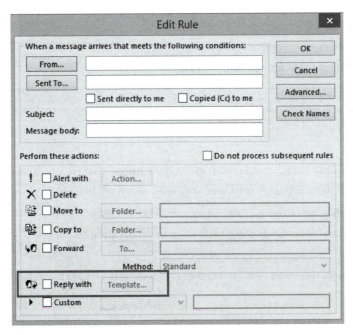

2. Writing skills

Here are some guidelines for writing auto-replies.

(1) Whatever your auto-reply is, make sure your reply will be suitable during some special situations and that your auto-reply is just aimed at a specific group of people or

existing just in a certain period.

(2) Remember to craft an auto-reply that's warm, personal, and informative.

(3) Write a strong subject line. The subject conveys the main point of the auto-reply. Is it a confirmation for an order? Is it a reminder? An acknowledgment? Make sure that the subject line is not too vague.

(4) The structure of an auto-reply can be as the following.

① Salutation. Usually "Dear Sir or Madam" or "Dear Customer" will be suitable for all senders since we don't know who it might be. We can also start with "Hello" to create a good atmosphere of relationship with our customers. If possible, make it as personal as you can—with modern mass email technology, it is easy to include your contact's name in emails, especially when it is the response to an initial request for support or to an order.

② Body part:
- Beginning part. Show why you set up the auto-reply.
- Middle part. Briefly state the information you'd like to convey. If it's an out-of-office auto-reply, your email should include other options for getting in touch with you to make it clear that the lines of communication are open.
- Closing part. Show your best wishes.

③ Signature. Write down your full name, position title, department or company and contact information.

Section 2 Samples

Sample 1 auto-reply for customer service

Subject: We Got It—Re: Scooters[1]
Dear Customer,[2] Thanks for reaching out! This is just to let you know that we received your email and will get back to you with a response as soon as possible. From 9:00 a.m. to 6:00 p.m. from Monday to Friday, you may receive a reply usually within a couple of hours. Evenings and weekends may take us a little bit longer.[3] If you have general questions about scooters, check out our website for product catalogs and answers to FAQs.[4] If you have any additional information that you think will help us to assist you, please feel free to reply to this email.

> Cheers,⁵
> Fred

Comments

1. 这是一封负责处理客户询盘的客服人员设置的自动回复。邮件主题中，"We got it"后面接对方的邮件标题，表示已收到对方的这封邮件。这种自动回复适用于每天收到的咨询邮件太多，没法第一时间回复的情况。如果客服人员能很快处理，则最好不要设置自动回复。

2. 因为回复的对象都是客户或潜在客户，因此称呼是"Dear Customer"。

3. 感谢对方的电子邮件，确认收到。告诉对方大概什么时候能收到具体的回复。

4. 引导客户可以先去浏览常见问题解答，使客户有机会第一时间得到相关信息。这里可以直接链接到公司网站的 FAQ 版块。

5. 从标题到正文，可看出本邮件较为非正式，这里结束敬语也选择了非正式的"Cheers"。

Sample 2 auto reply for customer service

> Dear esteemed customer,
>
> Thank you for choosing to do business with us. We have received your email but we have loads of inquiries to attend to. It will take us about three days to get across to you on inquiries concerning our sales promotions.
>
> However, if your inquiry needs urgent attention, you can contact our 24-hour customer care at 86 444-560-622.
>
> Sincerely,
> Ann Wang
> Bolton Limited

Core Vocabulary

esteemed	*adj.* 受尊敬的，受敬重的
loads of	大量，许多

Sample 3 auto-reply to an online order

> Hello Peter!¹
>
> Thank you for your order. We strive to process orders in 6 hours, and we will let you know when your order has been processed.²

While you wait, you can take a look at our Frequently Asked Questions.

Or, if your request is more urgent, feel free to give us a call at 86 13512345678.³

Here are some other home appliances you might find interesting.⁴

  -[1300W 5L stand mixer]
  -[2L stainless steel electric kettle]

Thank you again for choosing DOTTA for your purchase.

Alisa

Comments

1. 在某些邮箱系统中,可通过设置,在自动回复的称呼中加入收件人的名字。

2. 这里一封针对订单的自动回复。第一时间感谢对方的订单,告知对方什么时候能处理该订单。设置该自动回复的目的是第一时间向客户确认他们的订单已成功下达。如果客户是通过电子商务平台下的订单,还可以在通过平台自动发送的邮件中附上所订产品信息、送货地址等,以帮助客户再次检查所订产品及送货地址是否无误。

3. 提供紧急订单的联系方式。

4. 推荐其他客户可能感兴趣的产品,可以直接链接到所推荐产品的介绍页面。这是利用订单确认邮件,达到交叉推广产品的目的。

Sample 4 "office closed for holiday" auto-reply

Dear Customer,

Thank you for getting in touch.

October 1 to October 7 is the seven-day National Day Holiday here in China. During this period, I won't be answering emails as quickly as usual.¹

For immediate assistance, please contact me on my cell phone at 86 13512345678.²

Thank you for your understanding.

Best regards,
Alisa Chen
Head of Sales department
Greenhouse Fortune Company

Comments

1. 这是一封设置在假期发送的自动回复。需要写清楚假期时间以及假期期间如何处理邮件，是完全不看邮件，不经常查看，还是不能及时回复。

2. 提供紧急事项的联系方式。

Sample 5　out of office message

Hi,

Thank you for your email.

I will be out of the office from March 19 to 25 for a work conference. If your inquiry is urgent, you may contact Miss Alisa Chen (email: alisachen@qq.com. Mobile: 86 13512345678). [1]

I will respond to your email as soon as I can when I return on March 26. [2]

Thank you for your patience.

Best regards,
Fred

Comments

1. 这是一封设置在出差期间发送的自动回复。需要写清楚出差时间并提供紧急事项的联系方式。

2. 表明什么时候可以亲自处理邮件。

Section 3　Core Phrases and Sentence Patterns

(1) This is just a quick note to let you know we have received your message and will respond as soon as we can.

(2) Due to my tight schedule and so many engagements, I currently check my email on Monday mornings.

(3) Thank you for placing an order on DOTTA. We're glad to inform you that we've received your order and will process it very soon.

(4) We have received your email, and our support team will be in touch with you soon.

(5) I won't be in the office from April 15 to 20. Please expect a reply latest on Monday, April 21, which is my return date.

(6) I am currently on my annual leave and will be returning on September 12. I will not check my emails from September 2 to 11.

(7) You may refer to our FAQs at www.grindek.com/faqs for more information.

(8) If your inquiry can wait, I will surely respond as soon as I check my email on Monday.

(9) Thank you for understanding. I wish you all the best.

(10) If there is something urgent, please call Alisa Chen at 8613512345678 for help. Thank you.

(11) During National Day, if you have any consultation, please leave a message. I will reply to you at my convenience.

Task 2 Writing Notifications

Notification, as an official announcement about something that has happened or will happen, is very practical in business circles. It can target numerous subjects or readers, like the announcement of the new employee to clients, the notification of position adjustment, new company address, new price policy, new product launch or new business of the company, etc.

Section 1 Guidelines

1. Introducing a new employee to clients

When you hire a new team member who interacts with clients (e.g. a salesperson or account manager), you could send an email to announce the new employee to clients.

The new employee introduction email may include the followings.

- The new employee's name, contact details, duties, starting date.
- A brief description of the new employee's skills. Clients might wonder why you assigned a new employee to their account. Share key skills and professional achievements of your new employee to reassure clients that their contact is fully prepared for their tasks.

2. Informing clients of resignation or job adjustment

When you need to resign from a position in which you are used to working closely with clients, it is an expected courtesy to notify them of the situation. The best way is to send an email to clients. This will show the clients that they are trusting their projects with a good company whose employees have integrity, which in turn shows your employers that you are someone who holds goodwill toward them and deserves a great reference.

The email should include the followings.

- The date you resign.

- The reason you move on (optional). You do not need to go into great detail about why you are leaving; if you do not wish to disclose sensitive details, it is sufficient to state that you resign for personal or health reasons.
- Who will take over your responsibilities and his/her contact information.
- What the client should do if they have a question.
- Thanks for the client.

3. Self-introduction letter to clients

Introductions can happen for a few reasons: a new client may come on board, a new employee may connect with existing clients, a client may be assigned to a new team, and so forth. However, an introductory email always serves the same purpose: to tell the client who their new contact is and reassure the client that they are still in good hands.

This underscores the importance of an introductory email to a client. The email should include the following contents.

- Address the client by name, so they feel valued.
- Let the client know how to contact you.
- Assure the client that their level of service won't change (or will improve).

A self-introduction email to client contacts has to be professional and clear, and it must tell the client that you already know their needs.

4. Notification of price increase

It's important to let your customers know about an upcoming price increase, but telling them can sometimes be tricky. A price increase letter can be structured in the following way.

- Get to the point. It's best to just get to the point quickly-tell them how much their prices will go up, what they will be afterward, and when they take effect.
- Explain the reason behind the price increase. To make it clear that you're raising the prices to maintain the quality of the product, you should explain what caused the price increase. For instance, as some raw materials become increasingly scarce and expensive, companies are forced to increase the prices.
- Remind them that higher prices mean better quality. It can be confusing to customers why a price increase would be necessary, especially if they've been purchasing the same product for months or years. This makes it vital that you stress the importance of product quality. Typically, products increase in price to match higher operating costs, increases in hires, or prices of materials.
- List contact information for customers to reach out with further questions or concerns. You want to be sure your customers receive all the information they require. A lack of information could cause them to churn to a competitor with lower prices. Reassure them that they can always reach out if they have any questions or concerns regarding the price increase.

5. Announcement of an upcoming event of the company

If you would like to declare an important events happening in the business, such as a handover, it is helpful to send out a letter to vendors and customers. The letter is written in a formal and active note and is usually short, containing only relevant details.

It could be structured in the following way.

- Announce the upcoming event.
- Write about the progress that the company has made.
- Thank the recipient for the support and help in the past and express hope for continued support.

Section 2 Samples

Sample 1 introduce a new employee to clients

Dear Mr. Bernstein,

I am writing today to notify you that Andrea Liu is departing our company, effective September 28, 2019. We appreciate all the hard work that Andrea has done for us over the past four years. I would personally like to wish him the best of success in all future endeavors. [1]

As of September 28, 2019, Daniel Wang will be your contact with our company. Daniel has been with us for 3 years and has been successful in our sales department, reaching out to customers and proactively addressing their queries. We are all confident that Daniel will take on his responsibilities with enthusiasm and professionalism. [2]

Daniel will write to you shortly. Please feel free to reach out to him via email at danielwang@dotta.com or call him directly at 86 158124568789. He will be happy to answer any questions you might have. [3]

Best regards,
Jiehui HU(Mr.)
Manager of Export Sales

Comments

1. 开门见山告知客户旧员工的离职,表明离职生效日期以及对该员工的肯定及祝福。
2. 介绍新员工的姓名、职责、上岗日期,简短描述新员工的能力及素养,使客户放心。
3. 提供新员工的联系方式。

Core Vocabulary

depart　　　　　　　　v. 离开

endeavor	*n.*（尤指新的或艰苦的）努力，尝试
contact	*n.* 联系人
proactively	*adv.* 积极主动地
query	*v./n.* 询问
professionalism	*n.* 专业精神

Sample 2　resignation letter to clients

Subject：Moving on—Gao Jun of Dotta [1]

Dear Mr. Dillman,

Please be informed that I am leaving my position as the Sales Manager at Dotta Co., Ltd. on October 28, 2021. It has been a pleasure working with you throughout the years and I wish you all success and prosperity. [2]

Mr. Chen Yuhong will handle your orders and shall act as your first point of contact. Your association with Dotta will remain as solid and satisfactory as ever. [3]

Attached are Mr. Chen's contact details for your reference. I will be available until October 28, so please feel free to contact me as well. [4]

Gao Jun
Dotta Co., Ltd.

Comments

1. 邮件主题中，表明自己即将离开，开始人生的新阶段。收件人看到主题，可知哪个公司的哪个人即将离职。
2. 开门见山告知客户自己即将离职以及离职日期。表达对客户的感谢及祝福。
3. 介绍接替自己职位的人。
4. 附上接替人的联系方式，可附上电子名片。客户若有问题，也可在本人离职日期之前联系。

Core Vocabulary

move on	离去，继续前进
prosperity	*n.* 兴旺，繁荣，成功
solid	*adj.* 结实的，坚固的，牢固的
satisfactory	*adj.* 令人满意的

Sample 3 self-introduction letter to clients

| Subject: Introduction from Chen Yuhong of Dotta [1] |

Dear Mr. Dillman,

I would like to introduce myself as the new Sales Representative of Dotta. I have joined the company very recently. From my study of the records, I understand that you are one of our most valuable customers. [2]

We have been listening to what our customers have to say. Representatives like me are continually updated and trained on new products and services you need and expect. [3]

We have just added three products that have been asked for. Please check the attachment for detailed information. I would also like to discuss with you about these new products. What day is convenient for you? [4]

Sincerely,
Chen Yuhong(Mr.)
Dotta Co., Ltd.

Comments
1. 邮件主题一目了然,表明这封邮件是哪家公司的哪位人士发来的自我介绍信。
2. 开门见山地进行自我介绍,并表示自己做过功课,了解过客户公司的情况。
3. 表达自己有为客户服务的意愿及能力。
4. 顺便推销新产品,希望与客户预约交谈的时间。

Sample 4 announcement of price increase

| Subject: Pricing Changes on Batteries and Power Banks |

Dear valued customers,

We regret to inform you that we have to increase the price of certain goods due to the sudden increase in raw material prices. Since we still have a limited stock of raw materials, the price increase will not be made until November 2021. [1]

We have tried to prevent a price increase for as long as possible because of course, we want to provide the best products at a competitive price. However, the recent increase in the price of raw materials is now too great for us to absorb and we regrettably have no choice but to implement a slight increase on the items listed below.

- rechargeable battery
- power bank
- electric bike battery[2]

If you have any further questions or concerns regarding this price increase, please do not hesitate to reach out. Our team is more than happy to discuss this situation with you.[3]

Thank you for your understanding.

Yours sincerely,
Alisa Yang

Comments
1. 开门见山告知客户即将涨价,涨价的幅度、新价格的生效日期。
2. 列出涨价涉及的产品类别,解释涨价的原因,让客户明白涨价是无奈之举。
3. 客户若有问题或疑虑,请随时联系。

Core Vocabulary

absorb	v. 吸收
regrettably	adv. 很遗憾地
implement	v. 实施,实行
rechargeable battery	可充电电池
power bank	移动电源
electric bike	电动自行车

Sample 5   announce new production lines

Subject: New Production Lines to be Launched

Dear Mr. Bernstein,

We are glad to announce that we are about to launch new product lines and this all became possible with your support in the past years.[1]

Our new production lines are making us famous among our peers in the industry. Their cutting-edge technology will enable us to make out products of better quality more efficiently.[2]

> We hope for more solid business relations with you in the future, and as always, we are happy to serve your needs.³
>
> Yours Sincerely,
> Cindy Liu
> Sales Manager
> Huayuan Co., Ltd.

Comments

1. 宣布我方公司的重大好消息——即将安装新生产线,并感谢收件人一直以来的支持。
2. 说明此大事件给公司带来的积极影响。
3. 表达继续与客户建立坚实的业务关系,持续为客户服务的意愿。

Core Vocabulary

cutting-edge technology	尖端科技
peer	n. 同龄人,同辈,身份(或地位)相同的人,伙伴

Section 3 Core Phrases and Sentence Patterns

1. Introducing a new employee to clients

- I wish to introduce you to Gabriel Liu, our new manager in the client service department. She is assigned to handle your account.
- I'm reaching out to introduce to you Miss Yang Hua, our new Salesperson.
- Starting on September 21, Mr. Chen Kai will take over your account with our company.
- We are confident that Miss Yang Hua will tackle her new responsibilities with the same professionalism and enthusiasm that our team has continually shown in the past.
- I'm sending you this email to introduce our new sales manager. I'm pleased to say Mr. Li Qi was recently promoted to account manager, and we're excited to have such a great asset on our team.
- Mr. Li Qi has 3 years' experience in the field of sales. I'm confident he'll bring value to you and help you get the most out of our products.
- Mr. Li Qi will reach out to you soon for an introductory call. You can also reach out to him by phone: +86 13512345678 or email: li_qi@atk.com.

2. Informing clients of resignation or job adjustment

- I am writing this letter to inform you of my resignation from ABC Company and therefore your account.
- I am writing to inform you of my resignation from WES Co., Ltd. This, of course, means I will no longer work with your account.
- I wanted to drop you an email to let you know that I am leaving my position as the

Sales Manager at KK Inc. on September 11, 2021.
- I feel confident that you will not suffer any inconvenience due to my resignation, as a trusted colleague, Miss Yang Hua, will take over my responsibilities with your account.
- All of my clients are being transferred to my esteemed colleague Michael Smith. He has worked at TECK for over 20 years and I am extremely confident that you will get along great.
- The saddest part will be how much I will miss you as a client. However, it's comforting to know that my colleague, Barry Zheng, will take over my accounts, and so you will be in good hands.
- I have really enjoyed working with you during my time here and I wish you all the best in the future.
- I appreciate all of the cooperation and patience during the time I have worked with you.

3. Self-introduction letter to clients
- My name is Cassandra Chen and I am your new account manager at KOTTA. I am eager to work with you and your company to achieve more win-win results.
- If you have any questions or concerns, feel free to contact me via email or directly by phone at 86 20 1234567 ext. 224.

4. Notification of price increase
- Please note that we will generally increase prices up to 4% on all Passenger Car and Motorcycle products, effective Monday, June 14, 2021.
- Due to the increasing rise in crude oil, the retail price of our products will generally increase by 2%.
- This email is to advise you that there will be an increase of 9% in our Repair Parts taking effect on June 15, 2021.
- During the past year, we have seen ever-increasing costs for raw materials, manufacturing, and transportation.
- We are committed to finding ways of minimizing costs while giving our customers the very best products and services.
- We have attached a list of items that will be affected by the price increase and we would like to ask for your cooperation.
- As always, we are committed to providing superior products and services to you in the continued development of your business.
- We appreciate very much your business and continued support.

5. Announcement of an upcoming event of the company
- This is to announce that we expect to begin construction of a new plant in the first half of 2022, and it will complete in 2023.
- We are expanding our plant in Dongguan City, Guangdong Province. The plant,

where equipment is currently being installed, will open with an initial 3 000 square feet of production space.
- We are glad to announce that we are escalating our business line to its latest fifth unit with the help and kind support and patronage of our very reliable and regular customers like you.
- This is to announce the new product launch this weekend, October 11 to 12.
- For the sake of our customers and the advancement of technology, we have built the latest installment of our smartphones with cutting-edge technical specs and brand sparkling new features.
- This highly advanced unit will mark a potential turning point in the smartphone industry.

Task 3

Greetings on Special Occasions

On some special occasions, such as Christmas, New Year, Mother's Day, Father's Day, etc., westerners will convey greetings to their friends, colleagues, relatives or business partners. And when these people get married, have children, get promoted or release new products, it's also important to write greeting letters to them, the purpose of which is to contact these people in a timely and friendly way to enhance friendship or show a good relationship.

Section 1　Guidelines

In business, there is nothing more personal than sharing greetings with your clients and employees. This is the optimal way of building strong relationships.

Emails sent out on special occasions, such as holidays, birthdays of clients, festivals, are important to reach out to customers. Here are some guidelines.

(1) Keep the message short. Make it short and sweet. Keep their attention long enough to let them know you care about them.

(2) Keep the message personal. Keep your message personal by addressing each person's name. Addressing them by their first name will create a sense of intimacy. Do not use the same template for everyone. In addition, these messages shouldn't sound like a bad or cheesy advertisement. In fact, it's better if you try to hide the logos and slogans of your company.

(3) Send your messages in a timely manner. If somebody gets a birthday message three weeks after their actual birthday, this not only hurts your brand's image but would likely

annoy the client or customer. If you wish to send a congratulatory email to a client on his promotion, write it as soon as the promotion is public knowledge.

Section 2 Samples

Sample 1 holiday greetings

Subject: Holiday Greetings from Emily of Guangzhou Shipping

Dear Bill,

As a good friend and business partner, I wish you a happy and pleasant holiday to Hawaii with your family members in a few days.

Over the past years, we have established an unshakable relationship with your kindness and great care. I hope we can enjoy this friendly partnership in the days to come.

A pleasant journey and a wonderful holiday to you and your family out there!

Best regards,
Emily
Guangzhou Shipping Company

Core Vocabulary
unshakable   adj. 不可动摇的

Sample 2 Christmas greetings

Subject: Merry Christmas!

Dear Mark,

I would like to wish you a happy Christmas in the coming days.

Much to my great delight, you have been a great source of support to us in expanding mutually beneficial business and good cooperation between us in the past years. Millions of thanks to your continued concern and trust.

My sincerest wishes to you and your happy family. Merry Christmas once again.

Best regards,
Wang Qiang
Fortune Summit

Core Vocabulary

source   *n.* 来源

beneficial   *adj.* 有益的

Sample 3 New Year greetings

Dear Ms. Cooke,

With the year 2021, also the Chinese New Year of the Ox approaching, I wish you a lucky and successful new year.

We are so grateful for your continued support and friendship, and we look forward to working together in the new year.

May the joy of the holiday be with you in the upcoming 2021.

Best regards,
Liao Wen

Core Vocabulary

Chinese New Year of the Ox   中国的牛年

Sample 4 a happy birthday message

Subject: Anna, Happy Birthday!

Dear Anna,

Wishing you all the best on your birthday, and everything wonderful in the year ahead. Our business has been on the up-and-up because of great clients like you. On your special day, we have just two strong and sincere words for you—Thank You.

Sincerely,
Tina Liu

Core Vocabulary

on the up-and-up   越来越好

Module 11 Miscellaneous Correspondence
模块 11 其他函电

Sample 5 congratulations on a promotion

Subject: Congratulations from Gemma

Dear Julie,

I heard from Jeff that you were promoted to Vice President.[1] Congratulations! It's terrific to see that your hard work and achievements have been recognized.[2]

I'm thrilled to hear about your new role, and I'm glad we'll work closely together on upcoming projects.

Best,
Gemma

Comments

1. 说明你是如何知道对方升职的,可能是由共同的朋友告知,或者是看到了对方社交平台上公开的信息,这使你的祝贺显得不那么唐突。

2. 赞扬收件人的能力和成绩,表示这次晋升是对方努力的结果,你为其感到高兴。

Section 3 Core Phrases and Sentence Patterns

- I would like to extend my cordial greetings to you on this holiday.
- On the occasion of Christmas, I would like to extend my warmest greetings to you.
- I'd like to wish you-our cherished client and friend, a very happy birthday.
- Looking back on the past year, we see just how lucky we are to have people like you supporting us. Thank you so much for helping to shape our business. Happy Holiday.
- Thank you for making our jobs so enjoyable. We appreciate working with you and wish you a very happy, lucky and prosperous New Year.
- Happy the Chinese Lunar New Year of the Ox.
- Wish you every success in your business and career in the years ahead.
- May the days ahead of you be filled with prosperity, great health and above all joy in its truest and purest form. Happy birthday!
- On the occasion of your birthday, I wish you prosperity, good health and all the happiness that the room in your heart can hold. Happy birthday!
- May you be happy every day and forever young.
- Thanks for all your support and valuable business in 2020. We hope for a lot more fruitful results in 2021.
- With 2020 coming to a close, we want to reach out and send our best wishes to you!

- I hope that 2021 holds success and good fortune in any endeavour you pursue.
- It has been a pleasure getting to know you and your organization this year.
- We couldn't say that the work is easy if it wasn't for your constant effort and commitment.
- It is a pleasure to do business with you. Thank you for all the work and trust in us.
- As someone so dedicated and hardworking, you deserve this recognition and responsibility. And the position deserves someone as outstanding as you!
- You have done a fine job there for many years, and you deserve the recognition and responsibility of the position.

Tips

如何邮件通知客户涨价

公司出于某种原因不得不提高产品价格,我们不得不硬着头皮给客户写邮件,告知涨价事宜。这种涨价通知邮件在撰写时要仔细措辞,力求使客户接受涨价,新旧价格能够顺畅过渡。可遵循以下原则。

（1）不要显示过于愧疚。我们宣布和解释涨价计划时,不需要过度安抚客户。写信时可开门见山,直言不讳。如果邮件中的措辞显得我方立场不够坚定,客户很可能会要求延迟涨价,或者为他们破例,甚至让我们取消涨价。

（2）解释说明涨价的原因。最好能用数据加以说明,告知客户哪方面的成本上涨了,是什么原因导致的,后续的趋势会如何,以及公司打算如何积极应对,给客户信心,以求得到客户支持。

（3）强调涨价带来的价值。向客户传递积极的信号,说明价格上涨可避免牺牲产品或服务的质量,涨价不会削弱产品的竞争力等。

（4）为涨价设置起始期限。期限最好设置为自告知日期起至少30天,为客户提供以旧价格购买产品的机会。这就要求涨价通知邮件要及时送达,如果等到最后一刻才临时通知客户,很可能让客户无法接受,引起消极反应。

Communication Laboratory

I. Translate the following sentences into English.

1. 由于本人辞职,销售事务请咨询王小姐,谢谢。

Module 11 Miscellaneous Correspondence
模块 11 其他函电

2. 由于近期工作较多，故若有紧急咨询，欢迎留言或直接拨打我的移动电话＋86 13512345678。

3. 在放假期间，有关产品质量的问题，请与售后部联系（电话：86 20 33601441）。多谢理解与支持。

4. 谢谢您的来信。我会尽快回复，给您带来的不便我深表歉意。

5. 您的邮件我已收到，我会在上班后第一时间回复您。

6. 很遗憾我公司别无他法，不得不小幅度提高价格。

7. 如果您对此次价格上涨有疑问，请随时联系我们。

8. 新生产线的尖端技术将使我们更高效地生产产品。

9. 很高兴与您开展业务，感谢您所做的所有工作和对我们的信任。

10. 我在这里衷心祝愿您和您的家人，幸福安康。

II. Write an email auto-reply based on the following hints.

1. Suppose you are now on a business trip to Singapore to handle after-sales issues. During that period, you will be fully engaged in your work abroad without enough time to process your email in time. Please set up an email auto-reply to inform the clients about this.

Subject

Content

2. Please write a notification to your client, telling him that due to the increase in raw material prices, prices of A11 Adaptors and A81 Couplings will be generally increased by 4%.

The price increase will be effective from January 1, 2022. Current price structures will be kept for all deliveries dispatched up to Thursday, December 23, 2011.

参 考 文 献

[1] 项伟峰．外贸英语函电[M]．北京：北京师范大学出版社，2015．
[2] 熊有生，彭枚芳．商务英语写作[M]．北京：北京师范大学出版社，2011．
[3] 胡新，黄玲玲．商务英语写作实训教程[M]．杭州：浙江大学出版社，2014．
[4] 刘杰英．世纪商务英语函电与单证[M]．大连：大连理工大学出版社，2014．
[5] 程同春，程欣．新编国际商务英语函电[M]．南京：东南大学出版社，2016．
[6] 郑志明．外贸英语函电[M]．北京：北京理工大学出版社，2017．
[7] 李卫，赵秀丽，刘丽妍．新编外贸英语函电[M]．北京：电子工业出版社，2017．
[8] 吴思乐，胡秋华．世纪商务英语：外贸函电（第四版）[M]．大连：大连理工大学出版社，2020．
[9] 林孝成．国际结算实务[M]．北京：高等教育出版社，2015．
[10] 毅冰．十天搞定外贸函电[M]．北京：中国海关出版社，2011．
[11] 唐伟，杨明远．外贸函电[M]．北京：经济科学出版社，2017．
[12] 王兴孙，张春锇，邬孝煜．新编进出口英语函电（第三版）（高级商务英语系列教程）[M]．北京：外语教学与研究出版社，2012．